Eight Obscene Plays from the French Erotic Theatre of the 18th and 19th Centuries

Translated and edited by

John Franceschina

BearManor Media

Orlando, Florida

Eight Obscene Plays from the French Erotic Theatre of the 18th and 19th Centuries
© 2021 John Franceschina. All Rights Reserved.

No portion of this publication may be reproduced, stored, and/or copied electronically (except for academic use as a source), nor transmitted in any form or by any means without the prior written permission of the publisher and/or author.

Published in the USA by
BearManor Media
1317 Edgewater Dr. #110
Orlando, FL 32804
www.BearManorMedia.com

Softcover Edition
ISBN: 978-1-62933-670-1

Printed in the United States of America

Table of Contents

Foreword — vii

Part One: Plays from *Le Théâtre gaillard* — xiii
The Bordello — 1
Vasta, Queen of Bordelleo — 33
The New Messalina — 51
The Pleasures of the Cloister — 67
The Intrigue at the Brothel — 103

Part Two: Plays from *Le Théâtre Erotique de la rue de la Santé* — 129
The story of the Théâtre Erotique — 131
Dollar Sign — 139
The Games of Love and the Marketplace — 163
The Grisette and the Student — 177

A Select Bibliography — 185

Foreword

Merriam-Webster defines "obscene" as: (1) disgusting to the senses, repulsive; (2) abhorrent to morality or virtue, specifically designed to incite lust or depravity; (3) containing or being language regarded as taboo in polite usage; (4) repulsive by reason of crass disregard or moral or ethical principles; (5) so excessive as to be offensive. Synonyms include, bawdy, blue, coarse, crude, dirty, filthy, foul, gross, gutter, impure, indecent, lascivious, lewd, libertine, nasty, pornographic, profane, raunchy, ribald, smutty, trashy, vulgar, wanton, and X-rated. By definition, obscenities trade on, or are self-referential to moral and social traditions against which obscenities can (and must) be measured; and, no matter how prodigiously the obscene seeks to strike out against or supplant morality or virtue, those values invariably survive and are often strengthened by being juxtaposed with lascivious discourse.

The oft-cited example of obscene theatre in world dramatic literature is *Sodom, or, the Quintessence of Debauchery* (1684) attributed to John Wilmot, the Earl of Rochester, in which a stage direction reads, "*Then dance six naked men and women, the men doing obedience to the women's cunts, kissing and touching them often, the women in like manner to the men's pricks, kissing and dandling their cods, and then fall to fucking, after which the women sigh and the men look simple and so sneak off.*" Along with graphic displays of heterosexual copulation, same-sex and incestuous relationships pervade the play's five acts; and the use of language long considered offensive by polite society finds liberal usage in the drama's rhymed iambic pentameter. Ultimately, the characters' licentious behavior leads to their demise (via a pandemic of syphilis) and an afterlife in the fire and brimstone of hell. For all of the play's ribaldry—and there is a great deal of it—a conservative morality wins the day, and *Sodom* emerges as a kind of cautionary tale, often considered by critics as a satire of the profligate habits of King Charles II and the lords and ladies that inhabited the seventeenth-century English Restoration court.

That obscene literature generally, and obscene theatre specifically, has often been justified as a means to demonstrate the wages of sin is a rationalization that can be traced all the way back to Aristotle and Horace, who validated the utility of theatre (to teach and entertain) even if its plots dealt with (though did not graphically portray) incest, patricide (as well as matricide, fratricide, and infanticide), pederasty, and a whole gaggle of antisocial behaviors expressed in language that often (and almost always in comedy) traded on scatological and obscene expressions. As late as 2010, Daniel T. Smith, Jr. argued in his dissertation, "Libertine dramaturgy: Reading obscene closet drama in eighteenth-century France," that "the sexual transgressions depicted in obscene plays might not only cause arousal, but also develop humorous social commentary on gender roles, aesthetic commentary on the value of theatre and classicism, and political commentary on the monarchy and aristocracy" (3).

The eight obscene plays in this collection are examples of French erotic theatre from the eighteenth and nineteenth centuries. The first series of five plays comes from the two-volume *Le Théâtre gaillard, revu et augmenté, 1776–1865* (*Bawdy Theatre, revised and expanded, 1776–1865*): from volume one, the three-act comedy, *The Bordello*, and the three-act verse tragedy, *Vasta, Queen of Bordelleo*; from volume two, the one-act verse tragedy, *The New Messaline*, the free-verse three-act comedy, *The Pleasures of the Cloister*, and the one-act vaudeville, *The Intrigue at the Brothel*. The remaining plays were found in *Le Théâtre Erotique de la rue de la Santé: son histoire* (*The Erotic Theatre in the street called la Santé: its story*) (1864–1866): the three-act vaudeville, *Dollar Sign*, the comedy of manners, *The Games of Love and the Marketplace*, and the one-act comedy, *The Grisette and the Student*. These three plays and *Vasta* are the only works in this collection that appear to have been performed. Production details are included with the translations of the plays. The four other dramatic pieces, though intended for performance, were not produced (for reasons that will become apparent when reading the plays).

While the plays in this collection ravaged the boundaries of propriety and decency established in French theatre production in the 18th and 19th centuries, they still maintained a heightened poetic language and artificial theatricality which, even in translation, may distance them somewhat from modern erotica. However, the graphic descriptions of fornication (both hetero-and homosexual), defloration, masturbation, fellatio, cunnilingus, flagellation, impotence, defecation, and venereal diseases—in brothels, bedrooms, and nunneries—appear as vital and (depending on one's proclivities) stimulating now as they did two centuries ago. In addition, the use of "ticket names" for characters ("Fuck-Six-Times," "Limp-Dick," "Cuntilda," for example) which reflected the practice common to allegorical and satirical drama, might still evoke a smile from some while actively offending others. The light-hearted and flimsy-plotted vaudevilles, combining dialogue, pantomime, singing, and dancing are of special interest since it is surprising to hear songs with overtly sexual lyrics. The opening of *The Intrigue at the Brothel*, for example offers the following example:

> My father's balls
> Are hanging to the floor,
> My mother is desperate
> To see them dry up.
> Sometimes she presses them
> To get the juice out,
> And rubs her buttocks with them,
> And her asshole.

These works offer an unapologetically coarse commodification of sex, though the reader will find that in several cases, the author found it necessary to defend his work by way of an apologetic introduction, or by distancing himself from the claims of authorship. Whatever the case, the social and sexual mores of France between 1730 and 1865 are reflected in the sexual discourse of every play. In *The Erotic History of France* (1933), Henry L. Marchand argued:

> The theatre has always been the best mirror of morality in any age. When life became more than free, the boards swarmed with frivolity and obscenity of every kind. . . . But no matter how far some had gone, there were still many poets and mimes who refused to say obscene things. However, in a small intimate circle there is no need for any inhibition, not even of the most extreme perversity. Hence private theatres were established in which no bounds were set to any word or deed. Behind the grated lodges of these small secret theatres, the noble ladies of finest society might witness the erotic plays which showed priapism and philosophy in strange mixture. . . . The wealthy lover of the theatre provided for himself a stage on which those plays that would gratify his own taste would be produced. . . . Very numerous were the revolutionary comedies directed against church, state and monarchy. In 1791 there was a public theatre at the Palais Royal where a so-called savage and a woman performed coitus before a crowd of people of both sexes. Finally, both actors were summoned before the justice of the peace and it turned out that the *savage* was some rascal from the suburbs of St. Antoine, and the woman a common whore who had earned considerable sums by such pandering to the pruriency of the public. (134–135)

Whether produced on stage, or written (as closet drama) to be read, whether designed as masturbatory inducements or admonitions to promote moral behavior, the plays in this volume offer an intimate observation of the values and behaviors of a society where venereal diseases were rampant, and prostitution and promiscuity flourished, in spite of the endeavors of an equally profligate government, and a periodically oversexed clergy. An untitled poem, published at the end of *Le Théâtre gaillard, revu et augmenté, 1776–1865*, sets the tone and philosophy of the society in question and offers sound advice to the would-be libertine:

Foreword

It is in vain that at Kythera an imprudent fucker
Thinks of probing the depth of a young cunt.
If he did not receive from heaven a vigorous cock—
If he doesn't feel the cum bubbling in his balls,
He is still held captive by his carnal desires—
For him Venus is deaf and Priapus is reluctant.
O, you then who, burning with perilous passion,
Run the thorny career of a good fucker,
Don't go wasting away on a fruitless cunt,
Nor take for love a desire to fuck.
Fear the deceptive baits of vain pleasure—
And frequently check your machine and your forces.

Part One
Plays from *Le Théâtre gaillard*

The Bordello
or
The Troublemaker Punished
(c.1732)
Comedy in Three Acts, and in Prose
by
Count Caylus

The authorship of this play is disputed by critics. Attributions include Gervais de Latouche, author of the History of Dom Bougre, Gate-keeper of the Carthusians, *according to Voltaire; Lancelot, the countess of Verrue, and Melon (author of the* Essay on commerce*), according to a note in a manuscript by the Abbot of Saint-Léger; and Count Caylus, according to Barbier. The tone of the preface makes critics lean towards this last attribution, although a bibliography of the works of Charles-Francois Racot de Grandval, fils, lists* The Bordello *as one of Grandval's early works. According to Henry L. Marchand, in his* The Erotic History of France, *Count Caylus was the founder of the Academie de ces Dames et de ces Messieurs, a club designed to carry out the doctrines of love and ecstasy through the facetiae and serious works of the passionate muse. The* Bordello *would certainly meet the requirements of Caylus's Academie.*

To the Reader

Morality is a bitter drug for which man has a natural disgust; strictly speaking, it is a pill that he swallows reluctantly, unless it is enveloped in some sweetness which, by flattering the palate, makes it pass more easily. It is appropriate to disguise morality under different but insinuating tastes, so that one receives it pleasantly while it produces its effect. As is often the case with certain remedies which, appearing to be very prejudicial to health, are those which contribute the most to preserving it, so there are writings which, although regarded as a subtle poison for morals, are the most apt to correct them.

Comedies are like this: their goal is to inspire the horror of vice, by showing all its atrocities. This is the design we had when we gave this play to the public; every man of sense, free from those prejudices of education which imprint on the soul what is called modesty, will find here both instructions appropriate to move him away from debauchery, and that happy mixture which takes stock of perfection :

Omne tulit punctum which mixes useful dulci
(*He gains universal applause, who mingles profit with pleasure*).

However, despite all the advantages that could be derived from the performance of this piece, it is clear that it will not be performed. It is not, as one can well imagine, that the police put an impediment to it (likewise, careful to protect the virtue necessary to the destruction of libertinism, one does not believe that they would have granted its approval, if it had been asked of them); the only hindrance will therefore come from the difficulty of finding actors who can perform with dignity, and do honor to the work, by rendering in expressive terms all the brilliance of the action.

Everyone knows that acting is a profession. An actor is one who, without listening to his own passions, without indulging in his thoughts, borrows all his art from the character he is creating. If illusion is therefore essential to the theatre, it would be necessary, in order to produce this comedy well, that the actors were really brave men, and especially the women really virtuous. "It's arduous and difficult!" The problem is not easy to solve. Where to find even someone to play the commissioner!

But what reception will the public give to this piece? It is expected that fools and hypocrites will vomit, at the first glance, a thousand expletives against it and its author. They will regard him as a wretch drowned in the abyss of the most frightful madness. Similar to those ill-tempered little runts, or neutered pups, that yap at a mastiff making its way without being afraid of their yelping, they will cry out at the top of their lungs, that a work stuffed with filth and obscene images cannot be read without a shudder. What! one will say to them, these impressions so natural make you upset? Are you unaware then that these words, these objects, which, in your opinion, pass for dirty and obscene, and which revolt you, are the instruments and the organs of human nature? The pagan philosophers made deities of them. Their mythology depicts Priapus as a monstrous penis, and Venus as a voluptuous cunt. Which of the two more excites a woman's desires, either to name a penis in her presence, or to show her a huge one? Is it more modest to pronounce the name of Priapus or to design him in the figure of a very erect penis? Whence comes this affectation, in the Pollyannas, to promptly ruin all these monosyllables: cock, cunt, by biting their lips and maliciously lowering their eyes? If their imagination finds them dirty, is it not because of the indiscretion of certain false devotees who render these objects criminal to them, by inspiring them with aversion for very innocent things?

After all, it is obvious that this precaution, among the French, to avoid the pronunciation of these words, is proof of the degradation of their morals. Do we see the other more polite nations falling into similar ridicule? Don't they call, in their language, everything by its proper name? Why, indeed, treat dirty and obscene what the ancients had in veneration? Did Horace, the politest man of his time, hesitate to say these lines:

Nam fuit ante Helenam cunnus teterrima belli causa.

(*Helen's foul cunt was the cause of the war.*)

I move on to the reasons which led me to present this comedy.

Who can better divert young people from going to the brothel than to paint a sincere picture of all the atrocities it produces? To succeed, it was necessary to communicate all the words that are uttered there, and anyone who writes in the style of whores, cannot help using these terms: bugger, fuck, cunt, cock.

After reading this piece, we hope that those who had the unfortunate inclination to frequent a brothel, will loathe a place where money, health and honor are so unworthily lost; we wish to see them admire Clitandre, Isabelle, and hate Valère, with his whores.

Happy, however, if a crowd of libertines and girls fed on prostitution do not shy away from the lesson we have proposed to teach them, and if, without considering the dangers to which they expose themselves every day, they do not make an effort to correct themselves.

With regard to style, we will find it pure, and in some places, a bit feeble. I agree that I could have given it more strength, but it was necessary to accommodate myself to the different characters that I was dealing with. I tried to conform, as far as I was possible, to this precept of Horace who tells us that we must make an actor act and speak according to his particular character:

Intererit multum Divusne loquatur an heros...
Aut famam sequere, aut sibi convenientis finge, scriptor.
(Whether a god or man is speaking
Either follow tradition or invent what is appropriate.)

We know that a servant, a girl consigned to a shameful job, does not pride herself on the purity of language, and that one should not put words in her mouth as carefully chosen as in those who have had an education.

Characters

Valère, the troublemaker punished
Clitandre, the lover
Isabelle, the beloved
Madam Bru, the madam of the brothel
Margot, the servant
Bel-Air, the henchman
Valentin, Valère's valet
Beau-Soleil (Beautiful Sun), Clitandre's valet
Tonton ("Uncle"),

Desprez ("Desperate"),
La Poirier ("Pear Tree"),
Fanchon ("Kerchief"), the prostitutes
A spinner, from the parish of Saint-Sulpice
Bras-de-Fer ("Tug-of War"), an archer
A commissioner
Archers, in his retinue

(The action takes place in Paris, at a brothel.)

Act One

Margot. Who are you looking for, young lady?

Desprez. (*In rags.*) I would like to pay my respects to Madame Dru; a young lady in the provinces spoke so well about her, that I wanted to introduce myself to her.

Margot. Ah! I understand, you've come to ask for work, and you will have it, you are pretty enough for that; but you seem to me very badly dressed.

Desprez. I was involved in some trivial indignities, which really ruined me, and left me in the state where you see me.

Margot. But, pretty as you are, with good will, and what is more, tall and well built, your clothes absolutely reveal that you must have fallen on hard times.

Desprez. Alas! my lady, you're absolutely right. I was working in Lyon, everyone was chasing after me; at last, I was in vogue. A young man found me living with a good woman, who treated me marvelously; he took a liking to me, and I was foolish to love him in good faith; he put me in an apartment. Good fortune deserted me; I got pregnant. My lover was from a good family; his father feared that he would be foolish enough to marry me. This fear prompted him to have me locked up, and when it was possible for me to escape, I learned that he had sent his son away to foreign lands. Therefore, no longer wanting to stay in a city where my story had made too much of an uproar, I came to seek my fortune in Paris.

Margot. But, my child, your attire will ruin you, for you will have to rent clothes, and that will take so much out of your profits.

Desprez. I'll do the best I can.

Margot. If you are a good girl, and willing, Madam Dru could lodge you here. Also, for the moment, we don't have a housemaid: a soldier in the guards—friends of Madam Dru's henchman—defiled the one who used to serve us.

Desprez. We'll reach an agreement; but, please tell me how the young ladies are treated here, and all about Madame Dru.

Margot. Gladly. First of all, this house is very much in fashion today, and you will be instructed on how to conduct yourself with those to whom you will be introduced. In general, the least that one pays a girl in this house, is six francs, and, as in all the kingdom, half of it belongs to the madam, and four sols to the servant who fetches you and who gives you water to wash yourself. But if Madame Dru houses you, feeds you, and lends you clothes, you will probably only have twenty sols per practice. I know it's not a lot, but more will be added. Moreover, although you are pretty, you have already had a child. As for the two of us, because you see that I am the servant, we will get along well together if you feel like it; I'm a devilish housekeeper! Where do you live?

Desprez. Nowhere yet; I left Lyon with some small change for spending money; it paid my expenses, and I even earned some ecus on the trip, which I will gladly share with you for your protection.

Margot. Oh! my God, no; far from accepting what you offer me, I will lend you money if you need it.

Desprez. Thank you; I expect that God will reward your good heart. I arrived yesterday by the coach from Auxerre; I found a bon vivant, who took me to bed with him last night in an inn on the port; he left me this morning to go to his parents, and I came to Madam Dru; a cab driver gave me her address for the brandy I paid him.

Margot. All of this is going very well, but you are in no state to make an appearance. I hear someone; wait for me in the kitchen; if it's Madam Dru, I'll let you know. (*As Desprez exits, Valentin enters.*) Ah! It's you, Valentin?

Valentin. Hello. Is Madam Dru around?

Margot. No, but she should be back before long.

Valentin. So much the better, since I have to wait for her here. Is there any supper for tonight?

Margot. No.

Valentin. I'm very happy about it. And how have you been doing, my poor child, during the two weeks I've seen you here? Though I have come quite often with, or without my master, I have not yet had time to question you.

Margot. I'm not doing badly, because the work is rewarding; Madam Dru is very busy; she has old boarders who always give a lot to the servants; a great number of abbots also come; so, I earn enough money. I have no obligations or expenses, and what I make is for me.

Valentin. That's really very nice. If that continues, you'll be an excellent match! And Bel-Air? How do you get along with him? Isn't he still the watchman here?

Margot. Very well, I assure you; he's good devil, he protects all of this appropriately. But, will your master, Valère, be coming today?

Valentin. Undoubtedly. He even wants to have dinner here with one of his friends. Perhaps, before supper, he will play a game of quadrille.

Margot. How's he fixed for money?

Valentin. Not too bad. These days, we have bought a lot on credit, and very dearly, but in compensation, we have sold cheaply and in cash; the old misers are right that there is nothing so expensive as money.

Margot. What does it matter, as long as you have it!

Valentin. Yes, for you, but for me, it's not the same. I've got to leave this master. He has reached the limit of his wealth; I predict that everything will go wrong in the end. Moreover, he is, well, too debauched for me.

Margot. The decent man! It doesn't look like he's that way.

Valentin. No, my gosh. I speak to you very seriously; I want to make an end of it. Oh, that! Do you have something to give me?

Margot. Me, *gratis*, if you want.

Valentin. You, you're not what I want: it's too old-fashioned. You know that I only like my master's fucks, and you're aware that my greatest pleasure is to have them before him.

Margot. Just as you like; we will not have any dispute on that point. But I hear someone coming up, it's Madam Dru. Good evening, good rogue, I'll leave you with her. (*Enter Madam Dru.*)

Madam Dru. Ah! Hello, Valentin. (*To Margot.*) Has someone come?

Margot. No Madam. Only a very pretty girl came. She comes from the provinces to work in Paris.

Madam Dru. Where is she?

Margot. She's in the kitchen.

Madam Dru. I'll talk to her. Go and wait for me, and be careful that she doesn't rob me. Bel-Air hasn't come by here?

Margot. No, madam. (*She exits.*)

Madam Dru. Well! What is it, my boy? What brings you here?

Valentin. My master; I don't know what his plan is, but it must be considerable, for he gave me five louis—no, I said, four, to give to you.

Madam Dru. Mr. Valentin, you're a rascal!

Valentin. No, my gosh! I wouldn't want to deceive you; my tongue forked me, and the proof that I am telling the truth is that I will only give you four.

Madam Dru. Ah! There's a good fucking proof! By the way, what does he want?

Valentin. He wants you to reserve the green room for him, the one that overlooks the back and connects with this one, that one can enter by the bottom door.

Madam Dru. To hell with that! I don't want all that fucking mess at home. Why so much mystery?

Valentin. Honestly, I don't know.

Madam Dru. I don't want decent girls in my house, and I want you to fuck only those that I provide. I know what I'm giving, and I know where they come from.

Valentin. You can have your reasons; but there must be some bullshit in the air, since he's sending you four louis to get this room.

Madam Dru. All these buggers, like your master, are worth nothing to us. They make noise, they get drunk, they wake up a whole neighborhood, and all the neighbors complain.

Valentin. But my master pays you well.

Madam Dru. Ah! Fuck! Even if he would pay much more, is all that he gives worth the rest one enjoys with those shameful clerics, those bishops, those abbots, who pay double, who thank you on leaving, and who, silent in a room, leave you the freedom of your fully-occupied house? If there were thirty of them, we would hear a mouse stirring.

Valentin. If you don't want to provide the green room, then give back the four louis.

Madam Dru. Don't you know more or less what his purpose may be? Because, after all, I would like to earn this money.

Valentin. I swear, I don't know, like I said before, and I'm in good faith. But here he comes. He can satisfy your curiosity.

Valère. (*Entering.*) Well! How are you, Madam Dru? Anything new?

Madam Dru. You know very well, sir, the care I take to please decent people.

Valère. Did Valentin talk to you?

Valentin. Sir, madam has your money, but she's causing some difficulty. It's not as easily gotten as you might have thought.

Valère. Ah! of course! If the good lady Dru is difficult, then she is ill. (*To Madam Dru.*) And you, whom I have always known as such a ballsy woman, what can you fear?

Valentin. That's what I was telling her, sir, when you arrived. I represented to her the goodness of your patronage, because you are, without a doubt, the greatest libertine and the most debauched in the city.

Valère. That's true. (*To Madam Dru.*) By the way, do you, or don't you want it?

Madam Dru. What are you going to do with this room that you are asking me for?

Valère. Fuck.

Madam Dru. Who?

Valère. A cunt. What can you fear, since I'll take care of everything?

Valentin. Come on, Madam Dru; a man as wise as my master cannot expose you.

Valère. If she refuses me this room, I won't set foot in her house again in my life. Independent of the money I sent you for this room, I want to have dinner here tonight with one of my friends, and I want to have four whores.

Madam Dru. All right, then, we've got to do whatever that cock desires. Who do you want, Desjardins?

Valère. Fuck that! I'm tired of her.

Madam Dru. La Carnaut?

Valère. Oh my God no! She purses her lips while saying "fuck." In short, I want someone that I don't know: I want good girls, who like to drink, to yell their heads off; straightforward whores, in a word, who fuck well, give me my rest, and get drunk. But above all, don't give me Desvaux. She almost always plays the bitch; when someone says a word to her that she doesn't like, the hussy begins to get teary-eyed.

Madam Dru. Then, leave it to me; you'll be happy. I have a new piece that just arrived. I'll introduce you to La Poirier. That one's a good fucker; and you'll have two more that I don't think you've seen.

Valère. There's a good Dru! I feel my blood flowing. Go get everything ready, send for the girls as soon as possible, and let me give Valentine the orders for supper and wine. By the way, I forgot to ask you if you weren't related to that Madam Dru who figured out a way to put bells up her ass?

Madam Dru. Fuck you and your ass! (*She exits.*)

Valentin. This is going very well, sir. Without having to resort to questions, I can easily guess what you're going to do today: fuck, get drunk, and possibly sleep here. But this green room, I assure you, troubles me.

Valère. You will discover it's a charming project, which I will tell you in a few words. You'll have to go at eight o'clock precisely, to the Cafe de Dupuis, to look for Clitandre; that's where I made an appointment with him. You'll find him there, and you'll bring him here.

Valentin. Clitandre! And does he know you're giving him supper at a brothel?

Valère. Undoubtedly.

Valentin. I'm surprised; he is very astute and very much in love to play such a game. But, with all this, I still can't figure out the green room.

Valère. As he is in love with my cousin, and wants to marry her, he has to be kind to me. So, I requested that he come here for supper tonight.

Valentin. Very well! Sir?

Valère. Right! I have done so well that, since yesterday, because of the business that I raised with him, or the obstacles that I created, he has not been able to see my cousin Isabelle. In short, for two days he has neither seen nor met her, and for the execution of my plan, it is necessary that I occupy him this evening.

Valentin. But this green room?

Valère. I intend it for Isabelle.

Valentin. How, sir?

Valère. I was possessed, my child, by a violent desire to fuck a decent girl. I laid eyes on my cousin. You'll be fascinated by the way I prepared the whole business.

Valentin. Ah! Sir! You're making me tremble! What! To fuck your cousin, you're giving supper, in the same house, to her lover?

Valère. This is the conclusion of the plan. You know quite well that Isabelle is under the tutelage of Argante, an old bastard who torments her, and who does not approve of her marriage to Clitandre; you also know that Isabelle is passionately fond of this Clitandre. Three days ago, I overheard their conversation, in which she seemed determined to let herself be kidnapped. What did I do? I knew how to prevent them from seeing one another. I had her lover's handwriting forged, and the letter is written in its exact style. Clitandre declaims against Argane; he begs Isabella to give herself up to him, and to follow, at nine o'clock in the evening, whoever will give her this letter. He assures her that he is waiting for her in a coach at the corner of the street, but that he dares not appear in the house. Everything was successful; she received the letter, and here is her reply by which she promises to do exactly what has been proposed to her tonight. Imagine my pleasure; I am on the eve of fucking a virtuous girl, and I believe a virgin, if there is one in Paris!

Valentin. Sir, this whole project is so abominable, that you will be ashamed of having conceived it without having the pleasure of carrying it out.

Valère. The desire to fuck makes you think. Isabelle will therefore be taken at ten o'clock, and will find herself shut in the green room. During this time, I will be at table with Clitandre, whom the supper will make impatient; he will certainly leave the table early. Then I'll go find my cousin, and tell her she's in the brothel; she won't be able to doubt it by all that I show her. Dick in hand—I've always heard it said that a demure person resists even less than another—will determine it all the more, since I alone can bring her back to Argante, and make her peace. She will no less marry Clitandre, who will never believe that the adventure really happened, as long as it might cause a ruckus, himself having supped in the house which he would hear mentioned.

Valentin. Vice is very dangerous when it is unscrupulous. What a man!

Valère. Go get Clitandre, and bring him to me. I don't have to tell you that if you say a word about this, I'll break your neck. Stop by the *rotisseur*, because I want the supper I ordered to be ready for nine o'clock. Also bring us twenty bottles of wine: twelve of Champagne and eight of Burgundy. (*Valentin exits. Enter La Poirier and Fanchon.*) Come, my children, fly to me; But really, my good Poirier, here you are, well-recovered from your last venereal disease.

Poirier. Look at this bugger! If I had the pox, you gave it to me—Kiss me.

Valère. Ah! bitch, you bite. What is this hypocritically pious behavior? Come closer, kiss me too—Don't you know how to live? — Show me your cunt—Ah! Really, not bad—Come closer. (*He pulls some hair off.*) Even or not?

Fanchon. Ah! Bugger!

Valère. Oh! Look! She speaks. I knew I would make you say something.

Poirier. You'll be happy with her, she's a good girl.

Valère. I am waiting here for a friend of mine who is to dine with us; I recommend him, and I promise you a louis if you make him cum.

Fanchon. I will earn your money with a good heart, I assure you; just as well, I'm tired of an old bugger who was given to me at La Joli's, where I had gone by chance; he fondled me for over two hours, and my arm is weary of the time I spent jerking him off, and all for a fucking écu.

Valère. You're lucky! The one I recommend to you is young, but he's in the know.

Poirier. Too bad for him! Why is he coming here? Is he impotent?

Valère. Oh! that nay. But you, listen: when my friend arrives, we'll leave him with your friend, and we'll go into the fuck-room, and if you say at supper that I've fucked you twice since I've been here, I'll pay you well.

Poirier. Everything as you wish, but I think here comes your friend. (*Enter Valentin, with Clitandre.*)

Valentin. Here he is already; your supper will be served at the time you requested, and I am going to fetch the wine. (*He goes out.*)

Valère. Hello, my dear Clitandre. I'm charmed to see you at the brothel and, certainly, to spend the evening here with you. So, embrace these young ladies. (*Clitandre makes embarrassed reverences.*) Don't you see that he's just being silly! He's the bawdiest man and the greatest fucker in Paris. (*The girls leap at him.*)

Clitandre. Good Lord! Ladies, give me time to find my way around.

Valère. I will do better. Which one do you want?

Clitandre. Gosh! It makes no difference to me.

Valère. It's good to fuck before supper; we're freer at the table. I'll leave you with this one, and take my good Poirier in the other room. Come on, whore, come on.

Poirier. Let's go, fucker, let's go. (*She exits with Valère.*)

Fanchon. Well, do you want to do something?

Clitandre. Gosh, no. It's not that you're not pretty enough for that, and even that you don't make me hard—here's the proof. (*Shows his prick.*)

Fanchon. Ah! Sea dog, how hard you are!

Clitandre. Oh, don't touch it. You wouldn't advise me to expose myself here.

Fanchon. My faith! if you're afraid of the clap, you're right to be concerned. It's not that I think I have it, at least.

Clitandre. Eh! How do you know?

Fanchon. Alas! fundamentally, this is true, although I have never had any trouble, and have always been clean as a penny. But what the hell are you doing here?

Clitandre. I assure you that I came here in spite of myself.

Fanchon. Ah! I can see what it is now: you're gay, aren't you? You're pretty enough for that; but, my dear, there are too many of those male prostitutes, they're ruining us.

Clitandre. I swear I don't value them more than you.

Fanchon. Good! you sold me. Come on, do you want me to jerk you off with a finger in your ass? It'll make you cum.

Clitandre. No, thanks. I'd rather talk to you.

Fanchon. What the hell do you want to say to me? I don't know what to do. At least agree, dear fellow, that I'm a good girl.

Clitandre. That's right. Tell me, where are you from?

Fanchon. Orleans.

Clitandre. Have you been doing the job for a long time?

Fanchon. Almost two years, now.

Clitandre. Two years! You're becoming familiar with the work. Was necessity what prompted you to do it?

Fanchon. Yes, sir, as for the present. My father is retired, he was a master hatter. A dragoon officer made love to me two years ago, and offered to take me to Paris. That proposal turned my head; I accepted it. He placed me in an apartment, and looked after me for two months, after which he dumped me: what could I do but be a whore?

Clitandre. You could have worked.

Fanchon. That's easy to say, but you have to find work. You can believe that I would have taken anything available, because I swear to you that there's nothing I wouldn't rather do than the shit that I do here.

Clitandre. What? You're not happy?

Fanchon. Come on, you can't imagine the unfortunate situation of a girl who sees herself obliged, in order to live, to satisfy all the fantasies of the first comer fate gives her: the old, the stinking and the filthy, the impotent, or young people who mistreat you, and who certainly despise you.

Clitandre. They're right.

Fanchon. You're a fine fucking comforter of Job! My condition grieves me, and you make it even more terrible. Go fuck yourself. Leave me alone. I am the most unhappy girl in the world. At least let me cry for as long as I please. (*Enter Valère, Desprez, Tonton, and La Poirier.*)

Valère. Well! How are you, my dear Clitandre?

Clitandre. Very well!

Valère. Ah! Ah! What do I see? This bitch is all in tears. Does Clitandre have too big a prick, and it hurt you?

Fanchon. Leave me alone.

Valère. Who fucked me over with a bitch like this! Ah! By God! I'll teach you how to fuck and give you something to cry about!

Clitandre. Eh! Valère, leave the poor devil be. It's what I said to her that put her in this condition.

Valère. Okay. Okay. Let me kick her three or four times in the ass, and the same in the stomach, and after that, tell me about it. But believe me, let's kick this crying girl out. Look at all the good children there. (*Referring to Desprez, Tonton, and La Poirier.*) They're what we call whores. (*Slapping them on the ass.*) For that, Madame Dru served us well; let's all sit down to table, and join the freedom of wine to that of the cunt.

Clitandre. Let's go to supper, I agree.

Valère. (*To Clitandre.*) Take one under your arm, like I'll take these two bitches. Good—What! You're taking this cry-baby! I'm willing to forgive her because of you. If not for that, I swear, she wouldn't have had dinner at the table, and I would certainly have fucked her up.

End of Act One.

Act Two

Madam Dru. Ah! Here you are, my dear fellow.

Bel-Air. You see, my bollocks, I devilishly wore myself out doing business for the gambling den; that's what made me come so late.

Madam Dru. Don't you sleep here?

Bel-Air. Hey! Fuck! Wherever. — Is everything going well? Are there people?

Madam Dru. There's a supper for four girls and two gentlemen.

Bel-Air. Are those swashbucklers any good?

Madam Dru. It's Valère.

Bel-Air. Ah! Ah! It's the white wine!

Madam Dru. Himself!

Bel-Air. Who did you give him?

Madam Dru. La Poirier, Fanchon, Tonton, and a new arrival from Lyon by the name of Desprez.

Bel-Air. Does she know how to get on?

Madam Dru. She worked in Lyon: usually there's nothing to tell them, they come well-trained.

Bel-Air. And well-seasoned. Speaking of which, do you know that for you to have a Flemish girl, who is, Lord-knows, not badly-built, I crossed swords with this guy from Joli-Coeur? As we were drawing a blade, Sans-Quartier, our friend, whom you know, came by and separated us. Damn it! I was stabbed; I would certainly have had the edge on that bugger. He separated us and took us drinking; that's what made me come so late. He made us finger the girl, and decided that whoever won would pay the cost. Joli-Coeur won, and we choked back a pint on the end of the bench.

Madam Dru. All is going very well, and I am grateful for your attention. Come have supper and go to bed.

Bel-Air. I'm going—but, shit! Madam Dru, you're behaving badly. First, I need some money; second, you confide too much on your friends. What are these buggers for? They fetch you out of the hospital, but fuck! They don't prevent you from going there. Therefore, the great secret is to have friends in the police. And how do we get them? With money, Madame Dru; thus, either for them or for me, you have to put out money.

Madam Dru. Come and rest in there; let's fuck. We'll talk about business afterwards.

Bel-Air. Let's go—Hey! Isn't that Valentin? (*Enter Valentin.*) Good lord! How's it going, my friend?

Valentin. As you see, Mr. Bel-Air. Charmed to see you still here. Madam Dru's making you happy—she's well worth it, and does things nicely; isn't that true?

Bel-Air. Shit! She's a good bitch, and all this is managed quite well—(*Madame Dru gives him a look.*) Ah that! We're going in there for business; one day when you're free, come spend the evening with us.

Valentin. With all my heart, I promise you. Let me not hold you back. Go about your business. I have something to say to Margot, who's on her way up.

Madam Dru. If you need anything in there, just let me know.

Valentin. Go, go, don't worry. (*Madam Dru and Bel-Air exit. Margot enters.*) While they're at table, and all they think of is having fun—of course!—my dear Margot, do me a favor.

Margot. What is it?

Valentin. I don't think my master has fucked that new girl you gave him today, who he's calling La Desprez.

Margot. I don't believe so. Well! What do you want to happen?

Valentin. Let me fuck her, please. She makes me hard like a dog; I can no longer abide serving them. You know I fucked almost all of them before him.

Margot. Someday you'll get caught. But how do you want me to warn her and get her to come? She's at the table next to your master.

Valentin. Oh! (*Ironically.*) Really, it's a very difficult thing! A wink between whores is always heeded; if you choose, she'll understand perfectly, and most easily, what you want to say; she'll come out, under the pretext of something or other; you'll bring her here to me, and the bugger in there will have only my leftover this time. In short, I'll never forgive you, if you don't make it happen.

Margot. Don't worry, my poor boy. You have such a heart-felt hard-on, that I'm concerned for you. I'll do my best to bring her to you; but I won't have much difficulty in satisfying you. (*Enter Desprez.*) It seems to me that it is she who's coming here. Goodbye, I leave you with her. (*Margot exits.*)

Valentin. Hello, my dear child. Do you know that you are charming? Fuck me, please.

Desperez. I agree to it wholeheartedly.

Valentin. You made me hard like a dog while I served at the table, I couldn't stand it anymore.

Desprez. Of course! I saw it clearly, and that's what made me leave the table to come and find you.

Valentin. Right now, I've got to put it in you.

Desprez. Yes, but what if your master surprises us?

Valentin. What does it matter, shit! I would fuck you on a stone, I want it so much. Here, sit on top of me—very well—like this—place it yourself—Ah! Yes—

Desprez. Don't do it so fast, there's no rush. Aren't we fine like this?

Valentin. Yes—but, fuck! I'm cumming. Ah! fuck!

Desprez. On my soul! and on me too. You make me die of pleasure—Fuck me, dog!—Ah! shit! Someone's here; it's that fucking whore, Tonton.

Tonton. (*Entering.*) Good luck, children, this is not going badly.

Valentin. You see, we're passing the time.

Desprez. He gave me the pleasure of putting me on top of him, we were both craving it. Do you know how good it is?

Tonton. Oh! that yes, I know it well. I almost doubted this case. I saw that this beggar was ogling you, and I wanted to see what was going on. I'm bored like a dog in there. Those buggers drink and talk; as for Valère, he's half-drunk already, but I don't know who he's got today. He hasn't fucked anyone.

Valentin. You'll see that he's on a diet.

Tonton. Maybe he's got the clap.

Valentin. No, because he's drinking. It proves that we don't always get what we deserve.

Tonton. That animal which he brought back with him is a big impotent bastard, you have to admit; he yawns at the table, he doesn't know where to put his feet when he dances. Where the hell did Valère get hold of that wet-blanket?

Valentin. He's one of his friends who's not as debauched as he is. He's even a very decent man. I'm going to take a little look, though, at what they're doing in there.

Tonton. Oh! that nay. You won't go away like that. Fuck me. You think maybe you could leave me as you found me?

Valentin. What do you want?

Tonton. That you put it in me. Shit! I won't go away empty-handed. Those assholes in there may not be able to cum all night; besides, there are four of us, and when we're not so many, you get hard infinitely better than your master.

Valentin. Shit! I still have cum at the end of my dick. I can't.

Tonton. You will fuck me as if you had the pope's balls. You will put it in me, I tell you, or I will tell your master that I caught you here fucking Desprez.

Valentin. Be careful not to play that trick on me.

Tonton. Then fuck me!

Desprez. Go on, fuck her, my dear Valentine. This poor girl wants it. Can you refuse her a hump? Do it nicely, at your pleasure. To give you time, I'll go back to the table, so as not to make anyone suspicious, and I will leave you free. Farewell. Fuck to my health.

Tonton. It will be, Lord knows, to ours! (*Desprez exits.*) Who have you had today? You're very hard to please.

Valentin. Me, no. I just have to fuck if I'm hard.

Tonton. Eh! How many times did you fuck that little bitch who just left?

Valentin. Me? Just once.

Tonton. And after one time you're giving up! My poor boy, you're wasted, but don't worry, it's my business. I'll know how to make you hard. Please God, please the devil, whatever happens, I won't leave until you've shot it in me.

Valentin. So, let's do it.

Tonton. I'm going to sit on you; good, like that—Fuck me—Give me your prick. Ah! how soft it is! Take my cunt—Let's tease like that—Do I give you pleasure? Ah! guy, you're starting to get hard.

Valentin. Ah! Bitch! You would, I think, get the impotent Marquis de Gesvres hard! Let me put it in you—

Tonton. I knew quite well that I would live up to my reputation. But, wait a minute, it'll be better. Jerk off my cunt a little—yes—like that—

Valentin. Wait—you'll make me cum—

Tonton. Fuck! That's not on my account. Remain as you are here. We're going to do it doggy style—sitting down.

Valentin. Any way you want, as long as I fuck you.

Tonton. Don't put it in my ass!

Valentin. Don't be afraid, I'm not that kind of guy.

Tonton. Ah! Lord—how well you fuck. Am I moving enough?

Valentin. Very well—a little to the side—wonderful.

Tonton. Here it is, my Valentin—you know quite well, don't you, bugger, that I'm going to cum.

Valentin. Good for you.

Tonton. Ah! Ah! Bugger, I'm cumming—I can't take any more. Fucking dog! I'm fainting—

Valentin. If you don't let me cum, I'll knock you out.

Tonton. Don't be afraid. Fuck with confidence. Well?

Valentin. Well! well! Fuck! I'm cumming too—In gratitude, kiss me. Goodbye, I'm going to find my master. You'll always be a good fucking girl. Count on me to make our swordsman give you something more than the others.

Tonton. I'll follow you in a minute. I am going to wash up. Goodbye, my cock.

Valentin. Goodbye, my bitch.

Tonton. Go on, but don't go fucking around here! (*Valentin leaves. Isabelle enters, walking, and looking all around her.*) (*Aside.*) What do I see? Here is a well-dressed girl, and who has a really good manner: she looks only a little untrained. How often these hussies are good granaries for the clap! What we call real pickup-tricks. How does Madam Dru's deviltry work to find a new girl every day? I don't understand it at all. To get to the bottom of this: either I am seriously wrong, or there is some mystery in it. Let me approach her. (*To Isabelle.*) Hello, miss.

Isabelle. Miss, I am your very humble servant.

Tonton. Do you come here often?

Isabelle. This is my first time.

Tonton. Where did Madam Dru get hold of you?

Isabelle. Madam Dru? Miss, I don't know her.

Tonton. Come now! Don't be foolish. She says she doesn't know Madam Dru!

Isabelle. No, I swear it.

Tonton. Hey! why the devil are you here if you don't know her? You're going to tell me, perhaps, that you're coming here for the first time, and that you are looking for experience. It's a bit late for that. But tell me about it.

Isabelle. It would be too long an adventure to tell you what brings me here and would interest you only slightly. But, anyway, tell me, please, who this lady is.

Tonton. If you were talking to some trick, I would forgive you for speaking thus; but to me, it's mockery.

Isabelle. I beg you, by all that you hold dearest in the world, to get me out of the trouble in which I find myself and satisfy my curiosity.

Tonton. Madam Dru is the premier madam in Paris. So, you can see that you're in a brothel.

Isabelle. Good heavens! How unhappy I am.

Tonton. Well. What's appalling about this? If this is your first time here, you'll get used to it, as others have. Come, come, don't cry so much, we'll be able to console you.

Isabelle. Ah! God!

Tonton. (*Aside.*) There is certainly something underneath. I'll let her cry: above all, let's keep this adventure secret from the bawds who are dining here. In the end, she seems to me a pretty good fuck. (*Exit.*)

Isabelle. (*Alone.*) Nothing in the world can compare to the state I am in. My honor, my love both reduce me to despair. What! I'm in an infamous place. What! It is you, Clitandre, whom I loved more than my own life, who so injures me! No, I cannot survive all the misfortunes I am experiencing at the same time. But first of all, I have to get out of here. Even death, which I desire and to which I would surrender myself, would be an infamy: it would further confirm my dishonor. What! Clitandre, you condemned me to the horror of such a situation, you to whom I confided unconditionally, you whom I have always regarded as the most honorable man and the most tender of all lovers. Who can I trust now? But what do I see? O gods! It's him.

Clitandre. (*Entering, without seeing Isabelle.*) I can't stand it any longer! Too much horror, villainy, and debauchery reign in this infamous place. (*Noticing Isabelle.*) Ah! Good heavens! I shudder.

Isabelle. What! Clitandre, you can look me in the face?

Clitandre. Isabelle, is it you?

Isabelle. Do you fully enjoy, barbarian, the misfortune to which the love that I had for you has reduced me? At least don't push the cruelty any further. Trust that you have done enough to prevent me from surviving it. In the name of the strongest passion and the most tender love, take me out of a place where death, the only resource of the unfortunate, is prohibited by virtue. How can I not, in dying, have neither my death nor my dishonor reproach you!

Clitandre. Please the gods that I was the only guilty one here!

Isabelle. My misfortune is complete! What! you add to the horror of my situation by accusing me! But, alas! I am only guilty, ingrate, of having sacrificed everything for the love you inspire in me.

Clitandre. Why can't I find you innocent, Isabelle! I repeat again, I would sacrifice everything I possess to my desire to maintain my esteem for you. My shock and my pain at seeing you in this infamous place are proof of my tender feelings towards you. The very conversation I'm having with you painfully proves to me that one can only pass with great difficulty from love to hate, and that contempt alone cannot produce such a great change.

Isabelle. Overwhelm an unfortunate woman whose confidence in you—

Clitandre. Alas! What can confidence in me have in common with what is happening to me?

Isabelle. Can so many vices simultaneously have been hidden for so long under the exterior of virtue! What! I am still reduced to justify myself!

Clitandre. I would be only too happy, alas! if you could completely justify yourself.

Isabelle. (*Throwing him a letter.*) Here, cruel man, read!

Clitandre. (*Reading the forged letter.*) "You love me, I adore you; you know my integrity, so consent to my happiness, charming Isabelle. To hide the approach that my love is offering you, to which yours has subscribed, I spent the day yesterday without seeing you. Boldly follow whoever gives you this letter; he will lead you to the husband and the most tender lover." Oh, just heaven! I did not write this letter, my dear Isabelle; I was betrayed. Ah! My fury, my rage, my emotions cannot be conceived! However, what happened to you?

Isabelle. I followed the man who gave me the unfortunate letter; a coach was waiting for me at the door, I was hoping to find you there; but unfortunately! I did not see you. Despairing over this mark of contempt, I was taken to the room that you see, the door through which I entered was closed, and I was left alone. Worried, agitated, trying to clarify myself, I found this one open; I just saw an unhappy woman who clearly explained my misfortune to me, and you arrived.

Clitandre. (*Falling to his knees.*) Forgive me, beautiful Isabelle, for my unjust suspicions! Valère is the only one who could have insulted us so brutally; but his death will avenge us both.

Isabelle. How sweet it is to find one's beloved innocent!

Clitandre. My fury is at its height! However, we must govern ourselves wisely; your honor and mine urge me to get you out of here without fuss. Valère is drunk, I fear his insolence for you. While waiting for me to send for help, enter this room, where I will look after you like we do our most valued possession. And there we will accept the advice of the most tender and fervent love.

Isabelle. My fate is in your hands. I couldn't hate you, even if I thought you were guilty. My heart, then, gives itself to you more than ever.

End of Act Two.

Act Three

Valère. Valentin, will you come! Where is that guy?
Valentin. Sir.
Valère. Come on, then!
Valentin. My faith! sir, you didn't treat me too much as a friend last night, not only by making me sit down to table with you, but by making me drink too much: I have a headache this morning.
Valère. Everybody's hurting today. Come on, it's the fault of the hour, it can't be that of the wine. But are those rascally wenches up?
Valentin. There is one who won't get up so soon.
Valère. Which one?
Valentin. Desprez. Even though she's been puking all over the bed where we slept, she's still so drunk, that I don't think she'll be able to move all day.
Valère. She should have been relieved, however. I puked as much on Fanchon's throat, and that did me a great deal of good.
Valentin. It's apparently what you're congratulating yourself for that made them cuss so meticulously in there.
Valère. There is much to be angry about! Couldn't they do the same on me, since we were lying in the same bed? Fanchon may have been offended by the preference, she would have liked me to have given it to La Poirier, whom I had on the other side; but I'll give myself to the devil if I think of one rather than the other: so, they're wrong. Order me a ratafia, and have some coffee brought in. Listen, send the maid to fetch us all of this instead, and straightaway bring me my hat and my sword. (*Valentin exits.*) Hey! Fanchon, Poirier, come on, whores! Come see me! (*Enter Madam Dru, La Poirier, and Tonton.*)
Madam Dru. Who the hell is that bugger? Why, by all the devils, is he screaming so loud?
Valère. Why? because it entertains me. Ah! There you are, Poirier? Nice. Is Fanchon really angry? Ha! Ha! Ha!
Poirier. Lord! you must be the greatest swine on earth to laugh again after the filth and the infamy you have poured on this poor devil, who has no shirt here.

Madam Dru. What happened?

Poirier. He's been puking all over your bed; on my word, it'll be more than a week before you can use it.

Madam Dru. You have to admit that you're a big pig! Are you not ashamed?

Valère. I drink too much, I puke, this is quite natural. When I'm hard, I fuck, it's the same principle. What do you have to answer me?

Madam Dru. You're paying for my bed. (*Enter Valentin with Valère's hat and sword.*)

Valère. That's right, let's go. (*To Tonton.*) See you later.

Tonton. Ah! Fuck! Let me sleep in peace; I'm falling asleep.

Valère. Come on, it's to pay Madam Dru. (*To Valentin.*) Give me my sword; did you send for the coffee?

Valentin. Yes, sir. Margot's getting it.

Valère. Ah! Shit! By the way, Valentin, I'm in despair. Isabelle and the green room? Ah! Fuck me. I completely forgot about it. Why didn't you remind me?

Valentin. Faith, sir, I had other things to do. I didn't think about it any more than taking a bath.

Valère. What! haven't you seen anything? Haven't you heard anything, Valentin?

Valentin. Faith, no.

Valère. Go look in the green room; it would be very pleasant to find her still there. Go on, don't say a word if she's there, just call me.

Valentin. Sir, the door is locked and the key is inside.

Valère. Knock relentlessly. Push it in if you have to.

Clitandre. (*Opening the door and pushing Valentine.*) Get out of there, wretch!

Valentin. (*Running to Valère.*) Sir, here's Clitandre.

Valère. Ah! Of course! My friend, it's very nice of you to have slept here. I dreamt of you; We will have lunch.

Clitandre. (*At the back of the stage.*) Wretched man! Do you dare to look an honest man in the face?

Valère. What the hell's gotten into you?

Clitandre. I have here the most deceitful, the most villainous, the greatest reprobate there is on earth. It's you that I have here, traitor! (*Putting the sword in his hand.*)

Valère. But, Clitandre, you don't believe it. We have always been friends.

Clitandre. Me! The friend of a villain as despicable as you! Come on, Christ! Sword in hand right now. (*To the whores who scream and start to exit.*) The first one who'll cry and make a noise, I'll cut her face. Come on, Valère, this is your life, or mine.

Valère. But, Clitandre, listen to me.

Clitandre. I'm not listening to anything. I have my woman's virtue to defend, and consequently my honor. Moreover, I have to punish your falsehoods and the horror of your project. What! You also add to all your infamies that of being the greatest troublemaker in the entire world! Put the sword in your hand, rascal! Grab it, or I'll cut your face! Ah! wretch, nothing moves you. (*He stabs him with the sword.*)

Valère. Ah! Ah! Clitandre, you're quick.

Clitandre. Shut up, wicked man, you horrify me! Shit! Don't ever come near me, if you don't want to receive as much every time I meet you. (*He walks into the green room and closes the door behind him.*)

Valère. Oh that! Let's have lunch. (*To Valentin*) Go get us something cold in there. Come on, ladies, shit! I'll make you walk bowlegged.

Tonton. You?

Valère, Yes, me!

Tonton. I don't need anyone not to fear you and make fun of you. I won't even call Clitandre for help.

Valère. (*Putting the sword in his hand.*) Ah! bitch, that's too much.

Tonton. Approach, if you dare.

Madam Dru. Will you leave this girl in peace!

Valère. It doesn't please me. Here's the best kick in the ass you've ever received.

Madam Dru. (*Snatches his sword from him, and the whores beat him.*) Ah! Bugger!

Tonton. Ah! Dog!

Poirier. Vile jerk!

Madam Dru. Villain of Bicêtre Prison!

Valère. Valentin, take a log and knock out those bitches for me.

Valentin. Sir, I'm neutral in the second fight, just like I was in the first.

(*Margot enters.*)

Margot. My good mistress, we are lost.

Madam Dru. What! What is it?

Margot. The house is surrounded. The commissioner is here, following me.

Madam Dru. Alas! Everything is fucked up! What's happening? It's this fucking wretch that's causing us all this misfortune—Ah! Bugger, I'll beat you again before you get out of here.

(*Enter the Commissioner, his clerk, and his archers.*)

Commissioner. (*To the archers.*) Let all the avenues be strictly guarded, no one is allowed to go out, and let all those who enter the house be brought to me. Let an exact search be made under the beds, behind the tapestries; in short, let no attention be spared. (*To a guard, aside, who leaves after the order.*) Bring those I mentioned to you through the other door; when the orders I have given you are carried out, come and report. (*Aloud*) Let's take a look at all of this.

Valère. Shit! Sir, I am an honest man, and I have no account to render to a commissioner.

Commissioner. We'll see that in your turn.

Valère. My turn with those bitches? Good lord, you must be kidding!

Commissioner. Let's go. A pair of cuffs on the man, and hold him tight. (*To Madam Dru.*) Who are you, madam? From which country? What is your profession?

Madam Dru. Sir, I am the wife of a foreign lackey; my husband is now in England with his master. I am from Rennes in Brittany; I work in linen and lace for the court, and for several priests who will answer to you on my behalf.

Commissioner. Do you think, wretched woman, that I believe that beautiful story? Madam Dru has been on my agenda for a long time.

Madam Dru. (*Falling to her knees.*) Ah! Monsignor, don't take me. A scandal has never happened to me, and I dare assure you that no one has ever practiced their profession more honorably than I have done. I could even name you advisers in parliament, abbots and canons of your acquaintance, who will assure you that since they've been coming here, they have never been badly treated.

Commissioner. (*To his clerk.*) Get in a position to take the minutes. (*To the archers.*) Have you gone through the entire house? Bring me those you found. (*Exit archers. Enter Beau-Soleil.*)

Beau-Soleil. Sir, Clitandre has asked me to pay you his compliments, and to tell you that he will never forget his fundamental obligation to you.

Commissioner. Did he find the delivery coach I sent to the back door?

Beau-Soleil. Yes, sir, he found it; he has just left with a woman disguised under his cap.

Commissioner. That's going well. Virtue is safe; let's proceed against vice. (*Enter archers leading Bel-Air, Desprez, drunk, and Fanchon. The two whores are in their undershirts.*) Why, here's still more to add to the minutes. (*To Bel-Air.*) Who are you?

Bel-Air. Sir, I am a soldier in Champigny. I came to see the bawd when you arrived. I wouldn't have come here, lord knows, if I had realized I would meet you.

Commissioner. I hear—pimp—ta, ta, ta, ta, etc.

Bel-Air. Shit! Sir, the king's pay is so small, you have to have something to support yourself.

Commissioner. (*To the archers.*) Take him to the Abbey prison and get your receipt.

Bel-Air. But, sir, I haven't done anything.

Commissioner. I believe it, but a night is soon passed, and I promise to get you out tomorrow, if the depositions do not charge you.

Bel-Air. (*A Madam Dru.*) Goodbye, my child, take care of yourself. Send me the news when you can. (*Two archers take him away.*)

Commissioner. (*To Desprez.*) Who are you?

Desprez. Monsignor, I'm sick; my name is Desprez, and I have only been in Paris since yesterday; I come from Lyon.

Commissioner. If we say *in vino veritas*, we can believe her. (*To Fanchon.*) And who are you?

Fanchon. Sir, I would like to speak to you alone.

Commissioner. (*To the archers and all the rest.*) Move away to the back of the room.

Fanchon. Sir, I am the wife of Mr. Gueulard, a lawyer. He was one of the exiles, and as he is not rich, he left me nothing when he departed. I got to know this woman, who introduced me to friends who relieved me in my need.

Commissioner. Are you not ashamed, with resources and the ability to make an decent man happy, to lead a life so infamous and so detestable?

Fanchon. Alas! Sir, the horrible state in which I find myself reduced makes me shudder. In the name of God, don't ruin me, I promise you that this adventure will make me wise.

Commissioner. Come back everybody. (*To Tonton.*) And you?

Tonton. Sir, my name is Tonton.

Commissioner. Ah! Miss, I don't need your name. You change it so often, that the one today is not worth knowing. But were you not acquainted with fat Margot, last year, whom I sent to Bicêtre?

Tonton. (*On her knees.*) Ah! Monsignor, you're mistaken—

Commissioner. Get up. (*To Poirier.*) And you?

Poirier. I am La Poirier, that's all I'm going to tell you. You know that I'm a good girl, and that I have friends in the police.

Commissioner. (*To Valentin.*) Let's move on to this great parasite of imbeciles.

Valentin. Sir, I have the honor of being the valet of the brave Valère, and if I am here, it is the duty of my office which compels me.

Commissioner. (*Seeing an archer enter.*) What is this? What do you want?

Bras-de-Fer. (*An archer, who brings a spinner from the parish of Saint-Sulpice, who carries a letter to Madame Dru.*) Sir, she's a kind of servant who comes to bring a letter to Madame Dru.

Commissioner. Let her approach. Who are you, my dear?

Spinner. Sir, I am one of the spinners of the curate at Saint Sulpice.

Commissioner. Where does this letter come from?

Spinner. Sir, I don't know.

Commissioner. If you don't speak, I'll send you to jail later.

Spinner. Very well. Sir, it's from a bishop who will know how to get me out of trouble.

Commissioner. I forbid you to name him. Let's see the letter. (*Reads*.) "Send me, tonight, about six o'clock, the same person you sent me four days ago at Pantin. The carriage and she will be well paid, and I will send you your money tomorrow." (*He sits down*.) Well, that's it. Let's pass judgment. You, Fanchon, get your clothes, you can go out; but remember to be wise in the future, and not dishonor your family any more. La Poirier can go out too, let her pass. As for Desperez, she deserves some correction, but because it's the first time she's been caught, I forgive her. Go away; you won't be long perhaps without running the same risk.

Madam Dru. And my clothes, girl! Plan on returning them to me.

Commissioner. (*Silencing her*.) What?

Madam Dru. Yes, sir, she arrived yesterday with rags that aren't worth three cents.

Commissioner. Go away. I'm concerned with a similar discussion! (*To Tonton*.) And you, Mademoiselle Tonton, or fat Margot, as I have already had the honor of sending you to Bicêtre, and, since you know the way, you will be kind enough to return there, where you will be in the company you love, since we would certainly like to welcome Madam Dru there. But so that she may be in attendance with more dignity, her servant will follow her. (*To the spinner*.) And you, beautiful spinner, you will go to the hospital, where they will give you the most beautiful distaff in the house. (*All the women weep and cry like devils. To Valère*.) For you, sir, you will go to Fort-Bishop, where you will have few affairs. Your debts and your impieties will be carefully examined there, when you will have made a suitable reparation to Isabelle in court.

Valère. My God!

Commissioner. Let Madam Dru hand over the keys to the house, so that when leaving we can affix the seal. (*To the archers*.) Take all those cry-babies away; aren't the carriages at the door? (*To Valentin*.) For you, whose wages, I believe, are being paid by these proceedings, you can go in search of your good or bad fortune; but be careful not to fall under my paw!

Valentin. If the example of my master doesn't correct me, I deserve that you punish me as the most unfortunate man on earth.

The End.

Vasta
Queen of Bordelleo
(1773)
Tragedy in 3 acts and verse
By
Alexis Piron

According to Gaston Capon and R. Yve-Plessis (Raisonnée De Largot), Vasta, queen of Bordelleo, *designed in the manner of classical tragedy, and attributed to Alexis Piron (1689–1773), was supposedly performed. A note, published with the ballet that accompanied the tragedy even claimed that the main role was portrayed by Miss Raucourt (d. 1815) from the Comédie-Française, with Lekain (1729–1778), from the same theatre, as the male protagonist. Capon and Yve-Plessis add that this distribution of parts is all that has been substantiated: "Miss Raucourt's memory is quite extensive without any imaginary lubricities being attributed to her. As for Lekain, nothing in his life as a great artist and honorable man suggests such sexual deviations, such odious excesses. Vasta defies the briefest analysis. The names of characters themselves cannot even be transcribed. Is Piron really the author of this horror? It is certain that we recognize in it the work of a professional dramatist, and the sire of* Gustave Vasa *(1733) and* La Metromanie *(1738)." However, Piron was also the author of the famous* Ode à Priape *(1710) which prompted King Louis XV to veto his election to the Académie française. A few stanzas of the Ode indicate what turned Louis XV against him, and argue persuasively for Piron's attribution as the author of* Vasta:

>Of fuckers, the fable swarms:
>The Sun fucks Leucothoe,
>Cyrene fucks her own daughter,
>A bull fucks Pasiphae;
>Pygmalion fucks his statue,
>The brave Ixion fucks the clouds;
>We only see the spunk leaking:
>The beautiful pale and wan Narcissus,
>Burning to fuck himself,
>Dies while trying to fuck his ass.
>
>"Socrates"—you will say—"this sage,
>Whose divine spirit is praised;
>Socrates vomited plague and rage
>Against the female sex;"
>But for that the good apostle
>Did not fuck less than another.
>Let's better interpret his lessons:
>Against sex he's persuasive—
>But without Alcibiades's ass,
>He wouldn't have slandered cunts so much.

Characters

Vasta, *queen of Bordelleo*
Cuntilda, *her daughter*
Limp-Dick, *prince of the court*
Fuck-Six-Times, *foreign prince*
Balls-up-the-Ass, *Limp-Dick's confidant*
Dick-in-the-Air, *confidant of Fuck-Six-Times*
Banger, *captain of the guard*
Sucker, *Vasta's confidante*
A soldier
The High Priest
Crowd of people

The action occurs in the country of Bordelleo.

Act One

(*Onstage are Vasta, Limp-Dick, Banger, Balls-up-the-Ass, Guards.*)
Vasta. Yes, you fucked; your stupid expression
For a moment occupied my thoughts;
I thought that one was vigorous at your age,
And, without bullshitting, one could do it twice;
But since at the first stroke your limp prick
Misses its mark, in spite of my jerking ass,
That's the end of it. In the future, you will no longer fuck me,
Banger will recover so much lost time.
Limp-Dick. Oh! My soul is offended by this talk,
For, if by chance, you would misfire,
Would you blame the gods who gave you a cunt
More than one time too wide, and two times too deep;

The wind, which swept through that vast edifice,
Forced me to go limp at the edge of the uterus;
I thought I was being swallowed up; I felt distraught;
I was seized with fear, and my cum froze up.

Vasta. Are you fucking with me? What stupid excuse
Are you giving me? Is this the way you take advantage of me?
When a person has a real hard-on, nothing can stop him;
But one cannot count on a prick at ease.
Besides, you're a bugger, and if I believe my loathing,
Sir, you have trouble fucking a cunt.
Right now, choose: either the ass or the cunt,
Compensate for your shame, and avenge my insult:
That's the price for Cuntilda. (*Exit Vasta and Banger.*)
(*Enter Cuntilda and Sucker.*)

Limp-Dick. Ah! Goddamn! Princess,
You dare to call me limp in her eyes.
You heard it, Balls-up-the-Ass, it's enough to insult me,
Let's punish the bitch and avenge ourselves.

Cuntilda. Stop, Limp-Dick, how unjust is your anger!
What? Isn't it enough to have botched it with my mother?
Unfurling your indignant fury before her very eyes,
Disrespecting the place, me, my sense of decency,
You want to leave us. Ah! Don't carry on this way!
Ah! Cruel! Stop!

Limp-Dick. (*Going out.*) Go fuck yourself. (*Exit Balls-up-the-Ass and Guards.*)
(*Enter Vasta and Banger.*)

Cuntilda. Did you hear that? Neither my cries nor my tears
Could mollify him. Oh, height of misfortunes!
I've lost him.

Vasta. Get fucked, my daughter,
There are a lot of other heroes laying claim to Cuntilda.

The prince Fuck-Six-Times ought to be around here;
Go back into the palace. (*To Sucker.*)
You, follow the princess. (*Exit Cuntilda and Sucker.*)
And you, my dear Banger, come fuck your mistress;
Let's go into my bedroom.
(A soldier throws himself before the queen.)
Soldier. Ah! Madam, stop;
These walls are surrounded by fuckers and fucking;
The air rings out the cries of all their participants.
Prince Fuck-Six-Times, camped in front of our doors
To appear here with a dignified splendor,
Has joined battle with all the cunts, madam.
The Carmelites, the rowdy fellows who constitute his army
All have tremendous erections, and their chain-mail tucked up;
They've fucked the guard, and these bold men
Say that they want to fuck both the earth and the sky.
Vasta. I accept the omen, and I fly to their head;
I alone will confront such a tempest,
And if I fall, my friend, under the likes of those warriors,
I expect to match my laurels to their glory.
(Exit Banger and Soldier. Enter Fuck-Six-Times.)
Approach, Fuck-Six-Times; your rare courage
Deserves to be given a dazzling welcome.
That audacious manner, that noble vigor,
All make you appear to be an excellent fucker;
I hope to prove it and give you Cuntilda;
Today, Limp-Dick had to leave behind my daughter;
Your name alone, my lord, should make him tremble;
Can a bugger such as he stand up to you?
Fuck-Six-Times. Vasta, listen to me. Before a wedding
Here, unites my destiny to your daughter,
I believe I must explain myself, without beating around the bush,

About all the cunts, about you, about my love.
The cunt has no more charms after marriage;
And to change often ought to be its use.
Let us only speak of fucking, and the glory
And attractions of the cunt being celebrated in the palace;
Let the spunk flow through the streets
And fly through the air up to the clouds.
Vasta. Yes, Priapus himself has spoken through you;
You must dictate the laws everywhere you appear.
I wish to give an example of them to the rest of the earth,
Let me be the first to feel your blows.
Go, Sucker, go announce my desires,
And let us run to my bed to deliver ourselves to pleasure.
(*Exit Vasta and Fuck-Six-Times. Enter Dick-in-the-Air and Sucker.*)
Dick-in-the-Air. (*Taking Sucker by the arm.*)
Don't think about escaping me, even though you're an old bitch,
I'd fuck you in a second, be it in the cunt, or in the ass;
Dick-in-the-Air isn't made for hiding under a cloak:
That's only good for a masquerade.
Sucker. What! In spite of my age and my huge behind,
My lord, you'll dare to fuck me right here!
May heaven grant it to you and fulfill your desires!
I didn't expect benefits like that.
(*Dick-in-the-Air is about to throw Sucker across a bench; he is stopped by Balls-up-the-Ass, entering with Limp-Dick.*)
Limp-Dick. Stop, scoundrel!
Sucker. (*Getting up and going, saying.*) The devil take you!
Dick-in-the-Air. Eh! By what right do you trouble us in that way!
Why did you interrupt us in so sweet a moment—
And why did you tear me out of her arms?
Limp-Dick. Keep quiet.
I believe you to be the accomplice of a hated rival;

Get the fuck out of here, both of you, or fear my justice:
When the sun begins to shine tomorrow,
Let the walls of Bordelleo find no trace of you.
Dick-in-the-Air. I'm not at all afraid of that foolhardy command;
As the daily confidant to Prince Fuck-Six-Times,
Danger doesn't worry me, and I defy your blows.
Limp-Dick. Think about obeying me. I demand it.
Dick-in-the-Air. (*Going.*) Who gives a fuck!

End of Act One.

Act Two

Cuntilda. (*Alone.*) How now! I see myself reduced to lamenting my lover;
Limp-Dick is going to die! And that fatal moment
Will perhaps announce the victory of Fuck-Six-Times.
Will I be able, Limp-Dick, to survive remembering you?
Will Cuntilda be able to forget the pleasures
That you alone created in fulfillment of my desires?
That, on occasion, anticipating my tenderness, I saw you
Plunge me, suddenly, into the sweetest ecstasy!
Your finger, strong, yet delicate, exciting my bliss,
Quite often replaced your vigorous manhood;
I easily succumbed to my illusion.
No, nothing will be able to break a bond so sweet;
Nothing can tear you from the heart that loves you.
If you don't know how to fuck, at least you know how to jerk off.
Someone's coming. Let me hide the violence of my emotions.
Vasta. (*Coming out of her bedroom, disheveled.*)
Ah! I'm cumming again, and my impatience
Scarcely cools down in such sweet moments.
How appropriately you're named! Come, my dear Fuck-Six-Times,
Come soothe my senses, satisfy my tenderness;
Into your arms I crumble! What do I see? The princess.
(*To Cuntilda.*) What are you looking for, daughter, and why are you disturbed?
What are these tears telling me, and who can be causing them?
Cuntilda. (*Trembling.*) Ah! Mama, you know—no, I don't dare to say it—
Fuck-Six-Times, Limp-Dick—what blind madness!
Both of them at this moment—so long a story
Delays the relief—
Vasta. Eh! Fuck! Speak.
Cuntilda. Mama, they're in your hands, without the slightest doubt,
Limp-Dick is going to die!

Vasta. Eh! Fuck him up the ass!
God bless Fuck-Six-Times! All the rest don't matter.
Let your fucker die if it means saving mine!
And you, Banger, fly, protect the one I love;
Consider that if he dies, I'll take it out on you;
If it is necessary for Fuck-Six-Times never to be overcome,
I'll cut off your balls right up to your ass.
And you, who have displayed the fear of a coward,
Calm those useless emotions, and stop all your complaining.
How can you regret a fucker like Limp-Dick—
Without strength, without gusto, getting hard to no effect?
What can you expect from his flabby balls?
If he grows weary of masturbating, you'll grow weary of waiting.
(*Enter the High Priest.*)
Here comes the high priest. Let's consult him;
May the voice of heaven agree with my wishes.
Minister of the high altars of Priapus,
You, whom I revere and whose gaze gratifies me,
See mother and daughter kneeling at your feet,
To implore you on behalf of the destiny of Fuck-Six-Times.
Give me my prince, alas!
High Priest. Don't trouble your souls.
Fuck and keep quiet: that's what women do.
I swear by all the cunts in the universe,
By Priapus, to whom everyone must give way and bow,
That, today, Fuck-Six-Times, raised to the throne,
Will receive the scepter and the crown from your hands.
I swear to it, or let me become a eunuch!
I proclaim the fact to Heaven; my sperm guarantees it.
However, Priapus requires a sacrifice,
Let us beseech of this god supreme justice,
And that on his altars one hundred naked boys

May be immediately fucked by one hundred choice buggers.
That's what he wants. Obey, princess,
Come, let your hand uncover their asses,
Right now, assist in the enjoyment of the gods.
To prepare yourselves, both of you need to masturbate.
(*Vasta goes out with the High Priest.*)

Cuntilda. (*Alone, in despair.*) Who? Me? For Fuck-Six-Times who my soul detests
Would I implore a god whose deathly power
Could overcome the lover chosen by my heart?
Ah! Let this barbarous enemy die instead!
May he be struck down by a thunderbolt before my very eyes!
Would that I could see his prick and nuts ground to powder!
To see that vile fucker, with his last breath,
Fuck me for his punishment and die of pleasure!
(*Enter Balls-up-the-Ass.*)
What do I see? Balls-up-the-Ass! Ah! Comfort my soul:
What's happened to the prince?

Balls-up-the-Ass. He's fucked, madam.
That unfortunate lover, leaving this room,
Was sadly cursing the power of love;
Spread out on his bed, three bitches from hell,
Assembled around him, masturbated him slowly,
And that superb prick, seen at other times,
Filled with a passion so noble, ready to obey its voice,
Now soft, limp, its head lowered
Seemed to conform to his sad thoughts.
A horrifying noise and cries filled with horror,
Brought anxiety and terror to all the senses:
The door which had been placed under guard,
In an instant was broken down by a thousand butt blows;
It rattled with a crash and vomited before us

A ferocious bugger amid a flood of people.

His prick, large and thick, the audacity of which was extreme,

Craved to fuck the universe, and Priapus himself.

Nothing could hold back this wild fucker:

The ass he noticed shrunk back terror-stricken.

Limp-Dick, who saw him, took three steps backwards;

"It's Fuck-Six-Times," he said, turning to the rear,

"Let us flee the barbarous fury of my rival;

Let us abandon this place to that usurper."

Scarcely had he spoke when Fuck-Six-Times stopped him:

"Coward! It's useless to hold up my conquest,"

He said, and with a hand directed by Priapus,

He knocked him down at his feet, and with two whacks of his prick,

Without listening to his cries or his sad murmurings,

He made a gigantic gash in his ass.

For me, who couldn't watch that dazzling spectacle,

Without appearing, madam, dumbfounded and trembling,

I ran, I flew, in that terrible moment.

May the gods punish that horrible attempted murder.

Cuntilda. What horrors! I'm dying, and my heart, broken,

Torn apart by rage and sadness, beaten,

Mourns that lover who knew how to seduce me.

He was able to bugger without saying anything.

Let's never forget a mortal so limp,

And, straightaway, let us run—

Balls-up-the-Ass. Where, princess?

Cuntilda. To the brothel.

End of Act Two.

Act Three

(*Onstage are Vasta, Sucker, the High Priest, Guards, People.*)
Vasta. Let us give thanks, friends, to the god who protects us;
Limp-Dick is fucked; that flaccid sacrilege
And unworthy observer of the cult of Priapus,
Finally recognizes Fuck-Six-Times as the victor;
In falling beneath his blows, Limp-Dick surrenders to him my daughter;
He renounces forever the hand of Cuntilda.
Let's celebrate the glorious return of the champion;
Let the day be consecrated to the pleasure of fucking.
Instruct the princess about my supreme command:
I want Fuck-Six-Times to show her some tenderness
So that her heart will lose every memory of Limp-Dick
And prepare itself for a new pleasure.
Obey, Sucker, and as for us, let's fly to the temple:
When it comes to fucking, one has to set a good example.
(*Sucker, the High Priest, and People exit. Enter Dick-in-the-Air and Banger.*)
Dick-in-the-Air. Madam, at your knees, the prince that I serve
Brought Limp-Dick, weighed down by his fetters.
The atmosphere, which retained the uproar of his victory,
No longer forced him to see enemies of his glory;
When this traitor, enlivened by new emotions,
Seized Fuck-Six-Times by the middle of his body,
And then grabbing his balls from the rear,
In front of everybody, he fucked him on the ground.
Fuck-Six-Times got up, and with a furious expression,
"You betrayed me," he said, "but I swear to the gods
That, to avenge the disrespect you showed my balls,
This sword, right now, will cut off yours."
No sooner did he speak than Limp-Dick, defeated,
Saw himself a eunuch, madam, and fell on his ass,

"I'm dying!" were the only words out of his mouth.
Despite his treachery, his torture touched me;
Everybody was trembling, even his conqueror,
Who, turning his eyes away from the object of horror,
Sent me to inform you about this event,
Ready to obey the laws you might want to prescribe.
Vasta. Very well! Finally surrendering to my decrees,
Will Cuntilda admire the exploits of Fuck-Six-Times?
Speak. Did you see her?
Sucker. (*Running in.*) Ah! Excuse me, madam,
For the real sadness that fills my heart.
The princess is no longer, she died fucking.
Cursing the gods, in her final moment,
On the penis of a mule, at length, worn out,
Cumming, princess, she lost her life.
Vasta. I'm hearing about this so-called misfortune in the middle of a good fuck.
You won't see me display any sadness;
Becoming the mistress of the coward Limp-Dick,
From that day on, she had to give up my affection.
One day, my daughter would have dishonored my name;
I prefer her death to that shameful affront.
Instead, I'd rather the donkey fucked my entire kingdom collectively—
Than ever make anyone who resembles her!
We've been occupied enough with so vile a subject:
Thus, desires Priapus, and Vasta submits to his wishes;
May Fuck-Six-Times occupy our thoughts instead.
He's coming. Let's banish these baneful ideas.
Fuck-Six-Times. (*Entering and carrying at the end of a pitchfork Limp-Dick's testicles.*)
Let the flaming testicles of the traitor Limp-Dick
Ornament the dazzling vaults of the palace,

And serve forever to prove to the universe
That it saw his soul fucked inside out with this hand.
(*To Vasta.*)
Madam, you know that my rival, himself
Took my kindness by force, and that his extreme hatred
Sought to rip off my nuts with his hand;
He expected to take possession of my gallant gonads.
My arm knew how to punish him, and his two testicles
From now on will decorate one of your rooms.
I await from you my thanks, or my arrest.
Vasta. Ah! Don't expect any regret from me,
Although Priapus himself has struck down my family;
For you can't ignore that I no longer have a daughter.
She sacrificed herself to her resentment,
And death reunited her with her shameful lover.
I'm fucked. I said it and I'm saying it to you;
But it appears now that Fuck-Six-Times is reluctant.
Fuck-Six-Times. Me?
Vasta. You.
Fuck-Six-Times. No, no, never!
Vasta. Well, then, prove it to me.
Fuck-Six-Times. What do I have to do?
Vasta. Fuck and I'll believe you.
If you don't get hard, my lord, your senses
Might only be aroused by diligence:
I've assembled whores in my palace,
Let's wait upon their helping hands.
Fuck-Six-Times. Who, me? Need help?
No, I would deserve the most shameful torture
If my cock were able to relax for a moment
To the point of not being able to make you cum.
 I'm going to go to the bidet, and next to you, princess,

I'll spring up the moment you wipe your ass,
Fuck you, masturbate you into tomorrow morning,
The strength of my hard-on depends on your hand,
And if it's not enough, my dazzling vigor,
Without artificial means, and without help, becoming even more spectacular,
Will undertake in the eyes of the universe, to fuck
The priest, the priestess, and the god I serve!
Vasta. Fall to your knees, render him homage.
A god himself, would he be an even greater god?
Sods, cunts, asses, tits, get ready for him;
Fuck-Six-Times, henceforth, is your sole support.

The End.

Argument of the Ballet

The priestesses begin the ballet alone, and perform with dildos; they are interrupted by the warriors who create with them the thirty-two postures of Aretino and the pas de deux of the viola d'amore.

Verses addressed to the audience by Miss Raucourt, after having performed the role of Vasta.
Far from here? Ice cold fuckers
Whose cocks, afraid to go to two fucks,
Soften after the first, and desert the place.
Far from here! My favors are not for you.

Verses addressed to the audience by Lekain, who created the role of Fuck-Six-Times.
Youngsters who get hard at the brothel,
Always keep your cock in a cunt;
Fucking serves the country;
What does it serve it to be wise?

The New Messalina
(1773)
Verse Tragedy in one act
By Grandval Fils

Born in Paris in 1710, Charles-François Racot de Grandval fils debuted with the Comédie-Française at the age of nineteen, using the name "Duval," until his assured popularity with audiences prompted him to use his given name. The very handsome Grandval, so praised for his acting after his death, was, throughout his life, actively pursued by the fair sex. He married Marie-Genevieve Dupré, actress of the Comédie; but he soon parted ways with her, her behavior, in his view, leaving something to be desired. It was shortly after the death of his father in November 1753, that Grandval fils, came to live permanently with his mistress, actress Marie Françoise Dumesnil (1713–1803). To save appearances, he bought two houses in rue Royale on 17 September 1754, had fences built, separating his gardens from those of his mistress, and the lovers, thenceforth, lived closely and discreetly until Grandval's death in 1784. If the great tragic actress, Mlle. Clairon, in her Memoirs, *was not kind towards Dumesnil, she was, on the other hand, very laudatory concerning Grandval: "This charming actor, full of grace, wit and warmth, with whom what is called theatrical decency, has left the stage . . . having the wisdom to show himself only in roles suitable for his age, he has been forced to retire because of the disgust which his fatness inspired in the public of which he had been the idol." As a playwright, Grandval fils was an exponent of the "genre poissard," which celebrated the language and customs of lower-class merchants and thieves, especially those (called "poissard") whose fingers stuck to objects like glue. Occasionally, however, he would explore scatological and erotic subjects, of which* The New Messalina *is an example.*

The title, The New Messalina, *refers to the third wife of Roman Emperor Claudius (10 BC–54), Valeria Messalina (c.17/20—48), known for her insatiable sexual appetite. In his* Natural History *(Chapter 83), Pliny the Elder wrote of Messalina's challenging a prostitute to decide which of them—an empress or a whore—could outdo the other in servicing men over a twenty-four period. After virtually continuous intercourse, Messalina won, having had twenty-five tricks. The empress was fond of going to brothels, disguised wearing a blond wig and cloak, and enjoyed bringing a bordello ambience to the palace by compelling women of high rank to prostitute themselves while their husbands looked on. Claudius was tolerant of her behavior until he discovered that she had illegally married her latest paramour and that the pair were plotting to depose him. Quickly, and calmly, Claudius disposed of them both.*

The author to the reader:

One cannot reproach me here for having infected my play with dirty words and equivocal expressions. As far as I was able, I created a style that was clear and neat, certain that the reader, no matter how narrow minded, will find nothing beyond the door of his intelligence. For, imitating the tone of the great Boileau, I'm calling a cock a cock, and a cunt a cunt. The originality of my play forces me, in spite of my modesty, to say that it is an excellent example of its genre, that I find it so because it's mine, and that those who will have the bad taste not to applaud it, only have to toss it in the fire. That's what concerns me in advance. Farewell.

Characters

Couillanus, *king of Fuckland*
Messaline, *daughter of Couillanus*
Vitus, *prince and lover of Messaline*
Pinez de Villeprune, *prince and lover of Messaline*
Matricius, *prince and lover of Messaline*
Nombrilis, *prince and lover of Messaline*
Cunny, *follower of Messaline*
Several guards

The action occurs in the royal palace of Fuckland.

Cunny. Yes, this report is true and sincere;
Your father was seen on a nearby island.
Far from here for almost six years,
He's coming inside these walls to embrace his children.
What unfortunate falling-out propels you into despondency?
Wandering through this palace, always anxious,
You don't listen to me, and you close your eyes
Afraid of encountering the light of the heavens;
You have sorrow painted on your face:
Sadness looks bad on girls your age.
What's this? You're sighing. So, what's your secret?
Messaline. Ah! If I'm sad, he's the reason why.
You know Vitus, that admirable hero
Whom my heart adored, he's just miserable.
Cunny. How does he displease you, and what is this emotion?
Messaline. Alas! I see him only in the arms of death!
Undoubtedly you recall that, until today
When I saw him, I considered myself fortunate—
Because he had large and square shoulders,

A long nose, I could not have had a higher opinion of him.
On a bed of grass, he surprised me, sleeping,
He lifted up my flowing skirt with his hand,
From his trousers, he pulled out his cock—
And, in a word, Cunny, he put it in me.
What pleasure! What thrusts! Good gods! What joy!
Did Pyrrhus have more when he was burning Troy?
Never did my arms want to get free,
I sucked him, and jerked him off, and fucked, and came.
Well then, this Vitus whose extreme hardness
Fucked me, and fucked me again without appearing winded,
Today, under a spell that I don't understand,
He's softer than lamb's wool.
Besides, his prick, which seemed to live to fuck,
Couldn't pass through the lips of my cunt.
Yes, Cunny, that's my secret:
Ah! If I appear sad, don't I have a reason?
Cunny. Yes, madam, you are right to complain,
After an affront like that, what more can you fear?
But, in short, although it may be both cruel and extremely hurtful,
Don't collapse, and let so charming a cunt—
Be careful not to be flummoxed by shame and sadness,
To have felt the flaccidness of Vitus,
Wouldn't it be better to reward yourself—
Messaline. I understand, and I'll think along those lines;
I've been nursing far too long a faint distress;
From now on, I only want fucking to guide me.
All right, let flowing floods of semen
Succeed in filling all my lost time!
But someone's coming. Oh, heavens! Who could it be?
Cunny. Madam, it's Vitus. I see him making an appearance.
Messaline. Ah! Cunny, tell him about the state I'm in,

That all I can do is fly from him, and hate him! (*She exits as Vitus enters.*)
Vitus. She hates me, she flies from me. Ah! Bawdy princess,
Did you reserve that reward for all my tenderness?
(*To Cunny.*)
Tell me, why did she turn away?
Cunny. What? Because of you, my lord; don't you know why?
Don't brag about all your tenderness here,
You, you who thrust her all the way to limpness.
Vitus. It's not that astonishing, I swear, here and now,
That after nine times, a prick slackens a little.
Cunny. That's the whole reason for her overwhelming anger—
Ah! Perhaps, my lord, perhaps even if Vitus
Were a woman like her, after such an affront,
His brow would redden with a more shameful vexation.
But, avenge yourself, my lord, and choose another;
She's changing pricks and scorns yours;
Likewise, change cunts, and scorn hers.
If you like, I offer you mine.
Perhaps it's lucky that it has a great many charms,
A warrior, such as you, desires the noblest arms;
But consider, in seeing if it's large or small,
The change of cunt increases the appetite.
Vitus. I would follow your advice, if in this adventure
You had listened to nature a little less;
Undoubtedly, she directed you to speak to me like that.
I excuse your emotions; leave this place.
I could avenge myself for such an excess of boldness,
But it will suffice for you to leave;
It's enough to punish you all the more since
You wanted me to fuck you, and I didn't want to. Go!
Cunny. (*Aside.*) What contempt! Very well! I'll have you know
That your prick will fuck me, maybe more than nine times. (*Exit.*)

Vitus. Love, right now I feel your power.

You cheat sooner or later, and you make it clear.

Until now, I've only looked at Messaline

As a whore to amuse my cock;

In her, I notice attractions every day,

And the more I see her cunt, the more I experience love.

Cunny just offered herself; but she gets on my nerves;

I hardly feel that the pig will take her place,

For I love Messaline, and I'm going to strive

To discourage her by satiating her.

A Guard. Messaline, my lord, in her deep distress,

Desires that I remove everyone from the palace.

She's coming.

Vitus. That'll do. I'll leave her here

And not show her a face hateful to her. (*Exit*.)

Messaline. (*Entering with Pinez, Matricius, and Nombrilis*.)

  Come, famous heroes, all three of you take your places;

I know all of your exploits, but the choice puts me in an awkward position:

Yes, I desire that fate be decided only by the prick—

By the cock that will come into my bed.

But fate, what am I saying? How foolish I am!

No, we can only trust our experience.

The sturdiest one of the three of you

Will come into my bed, and fuck me the best.

All right, brave warriors, get your cocks hard,

Honorably bid for Messaline's cunt.

Enter the quarry, and display so much passion

That, between you, there's neither the conquered nor the conqueror.

Do you all submit to this common law?

Answer first, Pinez de Villeprune.

Pinez. I obey. I know the value of my cock;

Perhaps it is the smallest of the three,

But, what does it matter as long as floods of cum
Soak your cunt.
Matricius. Don't get ahead of yourself/
Let's decide which of the three of us will fuck her first.
Messaline. The first of you three to get an erection.
Matricius, Pinez, Nombrilis. (*Together.*) But we're all hard.
Messaline. Ah! What a happy omen!
I'll create another law, one more sensible.
Matricius, pull a few hairs from my cunt.
Matricius. I've got them.
Messaline. And you, Pinez?
Pinez. I've got them as well.
Messaline. Good.
As for you, Nombrilis; don't be scared of taking it,
My hair returns on the hour and springs up again from its ashes.
Now, count them. How many, Matricius?
Matricius. Nineteen.
Messaline. And you, Pinez?
Pinez. I've got four more.
Messaline. And how many were taken with his hairy right hand
By the silent Nombrilis, with his mouth sewn shut?
Nombrilis. I took seventeen, gentlemen; be witness
That if I don't speak, I don't masturbate less.
Messaline. Let's not waste time with frivolous talk;
We need action, not words.
On these premises, Nombrilis will fuck me first,
Followed by Matricius, and Pinez the last.
Let us go offer sacrifice to the god Priapus.
Follow me, Nombrilis, come enter the lists;
Let us lie down on this bed—I'm cumming already.
Are your cumming?
Nombrilis. Leave me be. Go. Go.

Messaline. What! Your cock's getting soft, the coward's shrinking;
I thought you had, at least, the strength of a Hercules;
Go away, leave me, limp-dick,
The devil take you and break your neck!
Come, Matricius, and take his place—
When I'm all on fire, why are you so cold?
Where is your cock?
Matricius. Madam, here it is.
Messaline. I'm falling. Good heavens! Charybdis and Scylla!
You can't get a hard on. God! What a disastrous upset!
(*To Pinez.*) What? In such a sweet field, you lack courage?
Pinez. Madam, I was hard, but I am no longer.
Messaline. Ah! It's too much in a single day to endure such rejection.
Lazy erections, flee. Get out of my sight!
Your pricks don't get hard when I'm completely nude?
Flee, I say, flee! Fear the impulses
That excite the passion of my resentment!
(*Pinez, Matricius, and Nombrilis exit.*)
(*Alone.*) Oh, rage! Oh, despair! Oh, Venus, my enemy!
Was this disgrace fated for me?
Did I incense your temple and your altar
Only to become the object of the feeblest of mortals?
Today, you can see those disgusting four misfiring
And not undertake a woman's vengeance?
Isn't it the cruelest affront to you,
That I've been finally reduced to frigging my cunt?
Avenge yourself! Avenge me! Seize the thunderbolt,
And let their flabby pricks be pulverized!
Oh, earth! Open up beneath their faltering footsteps!
Goddesses of hell, create tortures,
Every moment, go into abyss upon abyss
So, at last, they'll understand how the crime is punished!

In reversing for them the order of their destinies,
After their death, cause them to fuck whores
Whose syphilitic cunts, from the depths of their wombs,
Hurl at their pricks only offspring with the clap!
May filthy crabs cover all of their bodies,
May they always discharge green and yellow cum,
And may a burning canker, tormenting their souls,
Teach them unceasingly how to misfire with a woman.
(*Enter the Guard.*)
The Guard. Madam, your father has just this moment arrived;
To see him, the people are bustling about the bank of the river;
Some shouts are heard, but he's coming onto these premises;
For the moment, hide from him the troubled look in your eyes. (*Exit.*)
Couillanus. (*Entering.*)
My daughter, how sweet it is to me, after six years absence,
To be able, on this day, to enjoy your presence,
To taste the pleasures—
Messaline. Stop, Couillanus;
Your overzealousness is entirely unnecessary;
You're offended; shrewd fortune
Has not, in your absence, spared Messaline;
Unworthy of seeing you and approaching you,
Henceforth I must think only of hiding. (*She goes out.*)
Couillanus. (*Alone.*) What a strange welcome she gives her father?
That so sudden departure hides some mystery.
We'll discuss the subject with Cunny, who's coming.
To whom is the letter she's carrying addressed?
Cunny. (*Entering.*) My lord, it's for Vitus.
Couillanus. So why did your mistress
Fly away when I appeared? Is she afraid of my tenderness?
Her face is on fire, her eyes filled with wrath;
What is she doing here?

Cunny. She's fucking.

Couillanus. Fucking passes the time pleasantly;
I don't at all condemn such nice pastimes;
But must she give it all her time and attention?
It might be more virtuous if she fucked a bit less,
She might make herself a glorious name in history.

Cunny. My lord, many roads lead to glory;
The princess wants to have a glorious name:
Fucking is her virtue; it's the virtue of the gods!
Yes, the divine ones know of no other.
That's their sole pleasure, and it's our own as well.
Can we be condemned for walking in their footsteps?
When you want to, you can't.
You're quite mistaken, my lord. Fucking is the only glory
That can lead us to the temple of memory.

Couillanus. I give way to your arguments; so moving a discourse
Makes my cock stand up, and I feel it getting hard;
I'm going straightaway to my mistress.

Cunny. Don't go and give her proofs of old age! (*Couillanus exits.*)
(*Alone.*) Please, Cupid, protect my amorous design,
Make Vitus mistaken, and let him fuck me at last.
Look who's coming—if it he could only put it in me!
(*Vitus enters.*)
I've been sent to give you a letter, my lord.
Here it is.

Vitus. Let me read it.

Cunny. (*Aside.*) God of love, do your best
So that he suspects nothing of my trickery.

Vitus. (*Reading.*) "Adorable Vitus, if your heart still loves me,
Try to prove it to me right now;
I will come join you in this apartment
To swear to you a hundred times that my soul adores you.

My father is on the premises;
To insure that he doesn't come here and surprise us,
Lock up everything tight
So that no one can see us or hear us."
(*Going for his penis.*) Oh, extraordinary kindness! Adorable princess!
What! Your cunt is still interested in my prick!
And you, my cock, and you!—
Cunny. Good heavens! How pretty it is!
The cunt is thrice happy that will hold that bird!
Vitus. Why interrupt in such a way my training?
Alas! The next one is often uncomfortable.
And you, my prick, and you, the happiest of pricks,
Make, on my behalf, a generous effort,
And since I've never seen her satisfied,
By your intensified thrusts, do so well that, exhausted,
She falls limp, and confesses to me at last
That I alone was able to wear out her cunny!
(*To Cunny.*) Go tell her straightaway that, impatiently,
At the moment, I await the presence of her cunt. (*Cunny exits.*)
(*Alone.*) Cunny was eyeing you—you aroused her appetite;
It's true, I should have thrown her into bed—
What's it matter? After I've fucked Messaline
I'll be able to amuse myself with her dear Cunny.
Would my honor be offended by that?
My glory is to get hard, to fuck—that's enough!
Eh! How many are there, not one, but fifty
Who fuck the mistress, then the servant!
But my happiness approaches; someone's coming; I hear the sound
Of someone closing the curtains, hastening night.
Can my heart believe it? Is it you, my princess?
(*Cunny enters, in disguise.*)
Cunny. I won't deceive you in the slightest; I fulfilled my promise.

It is I, my dear Vitus.
Vitus. Masked! What for?
You're keeping something, and I sense—
Cunny. Hold on!
They're big handkerchiefs, around thirty-six of them.
Vitus. Four more, madam. One should have forty.
Cunny. I have them in the appropriate places, expressly
To dry my cunt: I am excessively clean.
Vitus. What precautions. My prick isn't strong enough
To starch your handkerchiefs like that;
You're mistaken. Look, madam, in other places
For more abundant cocks that can fuck you better.
Cunny. Until then, the traitor should swallow me up!
Fucking pleases him, but with my rival!
You wouldn't know how to get hard, traitor, and I understand it!
Very well! Enjoy me, then. Look, it's time.
See how my love has made me woo.
You remain surprised? I wanted to surprise you!
Your surprise avenges me, and soon, at this very moment,
You'll learn a much more important fact.
(*Enter two guards.*)
First Guard. Ah! My lord, listen.
Second Guard. It's I who want to say—
First Guard. Listen to me, my lord.
Second Guard. My lord, condescend to hear me.
First Guard. He doesn't speak your language.
Second Guard. He speaks gutturally.
First Guard. I give good accounts.
Second Guard. I have the voice of Legrand.
Vitus. Oh! You're making me deaf.
Second Guard. It's from too much zeal.
Vitus. With a single word, I'm going to end your quarrel:

(*To the First Guard.*)
You begin the story, and you, (*To the Second Guard.*) finish it.
We'll see which of the two of you is best.
Get chairs for each of us:
One must be relaxed to hear a recitation.
First Guard. Scarcely had the princess left these premises—
We see her leave, rage in her eyes—
She enters, emotionally, into the guardroom;
She says to the captain, tearing her clothes,
"Take off my dress." He does it. On a bench,
The princess immediately lies down and stretches out.
We devour with our eyes, her beautiful white thighs,
Her buttocks, and her breast, and her lovable haunches,
Her plump belly, and her very charming cunt;
Ah! My lord, I can't talk about it without getting hard!
"Let each one," she tells us, "quickly arm himself and get ready.
Today I'm celebrating the feast of Venus;
You won't have any difficulty, I promise you that!
Come, I give you permission, get hard and fuck me."
She speaks, and everyone admires her and gazes upon her;
And our captain, setting the example for us,
Fucks her, my lord, fucks her six times without breaking down!
We are then commanded to disrobe.
We disrobe; each of us, according to his rank,
Lies on top of her, rubs against her, and cums.
The number of fuckers doesn't intimidate her;
Holding her cavalier firmly in her arms,
Thrusting her ass, bringing together each buttock,
She unites valor with an admirable dexterity.
Finally, when each, following his appetite,
Has fucked, and fucked again, he washes his prick.
But, astonishing wonder! that one would hardly believe,

And which will never leave my memory,
The princess started to get up from the bench;
She makes an effort, but it is unavailing:
The cum which had spilled on the bench
Was so sticky on her back and her haunches
That she couldn't turn to either side;
Meanwhile, through our efforts, we lifted her up,
And I will swear to you, my lord, that never in my life
Have I seen a woman harden like that.
Second Guard. You ordered me to speak last,
I'll tell my story as neat as a penny.
The princess appeared charming in these adventures,
As much as an army general could be,
Who leaves an uncertain battle victorious.
All of a sudden, she entered her apartment,
And with the help of her ladies in waiting,
She washed her ass, her cunt, and each member as well.
After having thus completed her ablution,
She immediately makes a decision:
"Yes, I'll create," she says, "a noble enterprise!
Take my chariot out of mothballs,
Attach my six horses to it immediately;
I intend to visit the district of Mottas."
No sooner said than done; she climbs up and sits down,
She drives herself to Thalasse Street;
On her command, the chariot stops; she descends;
We're all surprised by the tears she sheds;
But, unforeseen woe that produced her tears,
She wants to cloister herself—
Vitus. Where?
Second Guard. With the Carmelites.
Making her farewells, she says these words to us:

"The virtue of my cunt got lost during my rest and relaxation.
I'm fulfilling a design worthy of my courage;
Until now, I've sampled marquis and page,
The Swiss, soldiers, grand admirals,
For them, in a word, my cunt was ordinary;
I have to end it: I want to try the monastery;
I leave the hay there to run for the oats."
Then she leaves us, and the monks, happy
Undoubtedly at that moment, fuck her, the best they can.
Her father, using ruthless apprehensions, futilely
Tried to turn her away from the Carmelite convent,
But she replied to him, opening her wide eyes:
"Then make me cocks that can get hard better;
I'm not at all afraid that being here is a failure;
I will satisfy them, I'll be satisfied.
What more can I wish for? My power is in my cunt,
And theirs is forever in their pricks and assholes.
But, what! Already the passion for fucking gathers them together;
Go away, my lord, go away, and leave us alone."
Her father abandons her, and says to her in anger:
"You want to live here, live; I don't give a fuck—"
Vitus. Good. I don't want to hear any more.
(*To Cunny.*) I offer you my prick; if you want to take it,
Madam, it's yours.
Cunny. I can't hate it,
And when you speak, I have to obey.
Vitus. Let us forget Messaline, and without going any further,
May we be left right here—Come.
Cunny. Where, my lord?
Vitus. To fuck!

The End.

The Pleasures of the Cloister
Comedy in Three Acts in Free Verse
(1773)
by
M.D.L.C.A.P.

In his dissertation "Libertine dramaturgy: Reading obscene closet drama in eighteenth-century France," Danield T. Smith, Jr. suggested that the identity of M.D.L.C.A.P., the author of The Pleasures of the Cloister *"is probably insoluble, but the combination of letters offers a variety of intriguing possibilities. If 'A.P.' means 'A Paris' (in Paris), that would leave only M.D.L.C. 'Madame de La Croix,' the owner of the brothel where* L'Art de foutre *[The Art of Fucking] was ostensibly staged [on 1 January 1841], is a possibility" (185). Whatever the authorship,* The Pleasures of the Cloister *trades on anti-religious tropes prevalent in erotic literature: a lesbian attraction between nuns; corporal punishment; sexual intercourse between monks and nuns; and sodomy practiced by monks with other men (either of the cloth or laity). Promiscuity without guilt in environments governed by the vow of celibacy has sparked the imaginations of authors and readers throughout the centuries and, in* The Pleasures of the Cloister, *Marton's fascination with the "sexploits" described in the erotic novel* Gate-keeper of the Carthusians *leads her to engage in similar erotic adventures on her own.*

Epistle

to the residents of the Convent of N. D.

You, whose dark retreat
Hides the tender attractions from us,
Who know little about the secrets
Of love and nature,
Take a look at this picture.
At this naive painting
I see a new fire shining:
The disturbance in your face
Detects an amorous desire;
Your heart renders, with a sigh,
To Venus its first homage.
Rascals, I see you blushing,
Less from modesty than pleasure.
By this innocent banter,
Kind ladies, let yourself be moved;
By reading this gallant work,
You will learn the art of softening
The rigors of your slavery.

Notice to Readers

This comedy had been composed for a society theatre; the difficulty of casting the roles properly has so far prevented it from being performed. Those of Agatha and Marton were easy to fill, and sought out by the young ladies. Those of Clitandre and of the Jesuit required actors of a certain strength, and no one dared to play them. Happier times will come. Although this play must borrow some of its merit from the performance in the theatre and the novelty of the spectacle, the author believed that a simple reading could be amusing. He carefully avoided any expression that might have hurt delicate ears. Why should we be afraid to look upon objects which are every day before our eyes, which most readers know by experience, and the details of which do not shock anyone in tales and novels? If one finds in this work some situations that are a little spirited, they necessarily relate to the subject. The author flatters himself that he has treated it with all the decency to which he was inclined. He will be happy if the fair sex, for whom he alone has worked, deigns to read his play and grant him a vote of confidence.

Characters

Sister Agatha, a novice nun
Mother Superior
Mother Theresa, mistress of the residents
Angelica,
Justine, lay sisters
Marton, a resident
Clitandre, Marton's lover
A Jesuit, lover of Sister Agatha

(*The action takes place in T—, at the Convent of N. D—, in Marton's room.*)

Act One

Marton. (*On her bed, the* Gate-keeper of the Carthusians *in her hand.*)
What trouble! ah! it's too much. Cease, charming book
From increasing my bewilderment.
An unknown delight takes hold of my soul,
A voluptuous flame
Ignites my loving senses.
Lustful Saturnin, how happy you are!
A daring lass, reckless Dainville,
Enjoys your charms without disturbing your sleep.
The approach of pleasure makes your heart less tranquil;

Gods! will I never have such an awakening?
What quick work! with your caressing hand,
You revive ten times his languid vigor.
I see Monique, in the grip of Martin's desires,
Desecrating the altar and the church:
As a maid close to her he disguised himself in vain;
The bitch, surprising him,
Flies to her mentor: a happy mistake
Thrusts her into the arms of the ardent Saturnin.
At your charming swimming pool,
Vigorous Celestine, why am I not a resident?
Subject to your lessons, supporting your efforts,
In amorous combat, you would see your lover
Weather the ecstasies of twenty united monks.
Sad convent! damn grate!
When will I stop being a child!
When will I feel a burning shaft
Enter my fiery bosom
And in its fast career
Forcefully dart it with a liquid flame!
I can't stand it any longer—what lively shivers!
What amorous throbbing!
I'm dying—

(*Throws down her blankets, and runs her hand under her shirt; one can guess her intention. In disarray, noticing Sister Agatha who is entering.*)

What do I see? Agatha! O, heavens, I'm lost!

Agatha. Hey! What, Marton, are you afraid to be seen by me?
You know my love for you;
Does it deserve such a thankless reimbursement?

Marton. Forgive me, I blush for appearing so naked.

Agatha. I read in your eyes a tender languor;
Where does this enchanting feeling come from?

Marton. This seductive book moved me deeply.
And I was trying with my hand
To relieve the passion that devours my breast.
Agatha. How amiable she is! How beautiful!
How I love this charming admission!
Victim, like you, of a cruel misfortune,
I feel the same torment.
While in these walls, an ill-fated slave,
Without a husband, without a lover, I will die languorously.
To the games destined for love,
You will bring happiness to a vigorous boy.
What a pleasure to kiss this emerging throat!
What a color! what freshness!
What dazzling whiteness!
Dainty feet, thin legs, and shapely thighs;
Let my impatient sight wander
Over those ivory globes rounded by Love. (*She looks in all directions.*)
Let me kiss a hundred times this charming froth
That tints the room with tender pleasures—
Marton, kiss your lover! (*She climbs onto the bed, and throws herself into Marton's arms.*)
Marton. Naughty girl, what are you doing?
You're making me uncomfortable.
What movements! Stop—
Your hand passing between the two of us,
Causes everywhere a burning sensation.
Agatha. Do like me, my dear child.
On your knees, hold me tight;
Push towards me—against my pressed breast,
Unite closely,
And let, by a gentle rustle
From the cave of Kythera,

The source of pleasure flow abundantly. Take heart!—Ah! I'm dying!
Marton. Me too, my dear friend—
Hold me, my love—my mistress—my life—Ah!
Agatha. How do you like my first lesson?
Marton. Ah! My dear, I'm delighted.
Agatha. Judge, by this sample,
The pleasure that a boy provides.
Marton. In these games I have little knowledge,
Teach me what it means to have a love tussle.
Agatha. When a vigorous young man
Surprises his lover in her bed
With a voluptuous kiss,
From the love in his bosom, he awakens fires
In the mouth of his mistress.
Slipping her his tongue with skill,
It flutters sweetly.
The beauty, blushing, responds to his tenderness—
Soon her cloudy eyes betray her weakness;
So, the rash lover
Grabs her breast, kisses it,
By sucking the budding button—
In her arms his lover squeezes him;
The rascal dismisses without ado
The obstacle that opposes their tender union.
He runs his hand over his half-naked nymph:
His finger, guided by desire,
Goes down lower and creeps into
In the secret lair of pleasure.
At the same moment the stimulated girl
Feels a gentle shudder.
She defends herself weakly:
The gallant changes his position.

And directing his winning dart,
He forces the narrow opening
Of the asylum that hides where modesty dwells.
This dart causes the beauty a stinging pain;
She cries, she wants to escape from his arms;
The cruel one does not listen to her;
He strikes the moaning nymph with urgent thrusts.
Marton. I surrender.
Agatha. Tonight, we will surely see
Both my Jesuit and your lover.
I'll inform the dear father with a note:
As far as Clitandre goes, it's your business.
Farewell. I hear someone, make yourself presentable,
And hide your book. (*She goes out.*)
Marton. (*On her bed, hiding her book under her mattress. Mother Superior enters.*)
Ah! Heavens! Hello, mother.
Superior. Hello, miss. How does it happen that today
I find you in bed at noon?
Marton. Alas! all night long a terrible migraine
Did not allow me to sleep.
When we're in pain, we're lazy.
Superior. You're lying; why blush?
Your complexion, fresher than a rose,
Is a silent witness testifying against you.
Well, what do I see under your mattress?
It's a book? Give it to me.
Marton. (*Blushing.*) Ah! I beg you, mother—
Superior. Your uneasiness, Marton, hides some mystery;
It's a novel, no doubt. Ah! corrupt books,
How you are wasting young hearts!
Let's read—*Story of dom B—, Gate-keeper of the Carthusians.*
This title promises a very pious work;

I'll browse through it.
(*She opens the book and sees an illustration.*)
Ah! what a horrible picture!
Abomination! What demon, stinking through this book,
Could defile the purity of this holy place?
Have you read this repulsive book, Marton?
Oh, heavens! and you don't fear
The fiery abyss opening under your feet,
Or the dreadful lightning from a vengeful God
Punishing your offences?
Tremble. I am the custodian of His power:
He orders me to punish you.
May a wholesome austerity
Cause a birth of repentance in your heart.
The Mistress of residents will soon be on her way here—
I'll inform her of this action,
And I forbid you to go out.
(*She goes out and takes the book away.*)
Marton. (*Alone.*) How unhappy I am! What should I expect?
Could I suspect someone would come and surprise me?
What! Is it a crime unworthy of forgiveness
To have a sensitive and tender heart?
How I hate you, black prison!
Where, because of false prejudices,
A slight pleasure, which is treated as a crime,
Places me, an innocent victim, in a tough position
For no reason.
Nevertheless, time is passing, and I must take care
Of the rendezvous that Agatha has arranged.
Let me reassure my worried heart;
Let the nuns be deceived;
I laugh at their punishment.

In my arms tonight I will hold my lover;
I'll teach him how to be delighted. (*She writes*.)
"Clitandre, if for me your heart is interested,
Come this evening to the place which will be prescribed for you;
The sister at the convent gate will lead you
Into the arms of your mistress."
I'll send the letter swiftly to his address.
Ah! Whatever fate awaits me on this day,
I surrender completely to love.

End of Act One.

Act Two

Marton. (*Alone, walking with great strides.*)
How slowly the day goes by;
I run, I go, I come, I languish waiting
For this sweet and charming night
That must unite me with my lover.
Voluptuous transports that Venus brings to life,
Tender outbursts, amorous languor,
Come crowding into my heart,
Increase the pleasures of the object I adore;
In these delicious moments,
His efforts will respond to my burning desires,
And in a thousand embraces,
Our souls and our bodies will merge.
(*Enter Sister Theresa, mistress of the residents, Sister Angelica, and Sister Justine, in conversation.*)

Theresa. Dishonor of this house,
Approach, guilty Marton;
Give thanks to our indulgence:
We were duty-bound to cast you out.
With submission, receive the correction
That will restore your innocence to you;
Offer, my daughter, with a good heart,
This penance to the Lord;
Happily, if you cry out, your bitter pain
Can disarm his anger.
For your fault, to heaven, to us,
Ask for forgiveness on your knees.
Lift up your petticoats and, up to the waist,
Uncover that impure flesh,
The object of heavenly wrath.

Sister Angelica, Sister Justine,
Deploy your discipline,
And each give twenty lashes
To this young libertine.
Marton. (*On her knees.*) Venerable mother, forgive me.
I admit my fault, and I am dismayed;
This is the first time that Marton
Had abandoned herself to temptation.
Be sensitive to my pain.
At your feet I swear to the Lord
That I will master this guilty flesh.
Forgive me.
Theresa. No, no, I am adamant.
Get up, Marton, compose yourself;
Lean over the bed. Come on, Sister Angelica.
Marton. (*Pulling up her skirts.*) Ah! Mother!
Theresa. No use replying.
Whip, sister; I'll be counting the lashes. (*The nun whips.*)
One, two, three, four.
Marton. Ah! Ah!
Theresa. (*To Angelica.*) Harder!
Marton. Ah! Ah! Mother Theresa!
Theresa. Five, six, seven.
Marton. Ah! Ah! Ah!
Theresa. Eight, nine. (*To Marton, who balks.*) Be quiet.
Or we will repeat it.
Marton. (*Warding them off with her hands.*) Ah! Ah!
Theresa. Endure it! (*To Angelica.*)
Hard, hard, sister: ten, eleven, twelve, thirteen—
Marton. Ah! Sister, ah! ah! ah! I won't survive this.
Theresa. Your cries, your tears are gratuitous.
(*To Angelica.*) Strike! Fourteen, fifteen, sixteen.

Marton. Ah! ah! (*Marton, struggling, drops a corner of her petticoats, and discipline breaks down.*)

Theresa. Hold on, there are three lashes missing.

Let's count them again, don't be upset:

Fourteen, fifteen, sixteen. Angelica, come forward,

And to whip more easily,

Hold her rolled up petticoats with your other hand.

Seventeen—put your back into it.

Marton. (*Feeling touched in a certain place.*)

Ah! ah! You're hurting me.

Theresa. Good. Tomorrow you will be healed.

Eighteen.

Marton. Ah! ah!

Theresa. Nineteen.

Marton. Ah! ah!

Theresa. Twenty. That's enough.

Sister Justine, you begin.

Justine. Eh! Mother, Marton has been punished well enough;

The poor child is all aflame.

Marton. (*Bowing down.*) Alas! Madam, in the name of God,

I cannot resist it.

Theresa. Please, shut up.

Twenty more lashes are needed.

Come, therefore, take your place. I want to be obeyed.

Quick, sister, whip; it needs to be done.

I will count softly with my rosary.

(*Marton takes her place, Justine whips her.*)

Marton. Ah! ah!

Theresa. Peace!

Marton. Ah! Lord!

Theresa. (*To Justine who is whipping feebly.*)

A little harder, my dear.

You're slowing down.
(*Justine whips harder.*)
Marton. Ah! ah!
Theresa. (*To Marton.*) What madness!
Hold your legs, please.
Marton. Ah! Heavens!
Theresa. (*To Justine.*) Strap her up, nicely.
Marton. Ah! ah!
Theresa. (*To Justine.*) Without cheating,
Sister, or without leaving this place,
We would perform the same ceremony on you.
(*Justine whips robustly.*)
Marton. Ah! My God!
Theresa. Hard.
Marton. Ah! ah!
Theresa. Good. Our business is complete.
Cover yourself, Marton, mourn your sin,
And don't return to it during your lifetime.
(*She exits with Angelica,*)
Marton. (*Lowering her petticoats.*)
Ah! heavens! I can't take it anymore. My back is flayed.
Justine. We have treated you cruelly, Marton;
If only, my daughter, I could have been able to shorten this torment!
Marton. Nevertheless, you didn't
Dust me less harshly.
Justine. If I had hit softly,
I would have been inflicted with the same punishment.
Once, on a novice
I exercised this cruel office—
Sensitive to her pain, I slowed down my strokes;
The prioress knew this and got angry.
They punished my piety: I had to ask for mercy,

I had to put myself in her place.
Assign, my dear, to necessity
My excessive cruelty.
Farewell. (*She leaves.*)
Marton. Flee from me, ruthless shrew.
I yield the convent and the nuns to the devil!
(*Enter Sister Agatha.*)
Ah! dear Agatha, come; do you know what they did to me?
Agatha. I know you were given the whip.
Let me see what condition that charming skin is in. (*She discovers it.*)
Ah! heavens! It's red and burning—
Let me kiss it tenderly!
Marton. May your obliging friendship
Bring me relief!
Sister Angelica and Sister Justine
Have applied to me, with nervous arms,
Forty lashes of discipline.
I am enraged. Tomorrow I want to leave this place.
Agatha. Far from moaning about your disgrace,
To the nuns you should give thanks.
Learn, young Marton, that vigorous blows
Make you more sensitive to the pleasure of love.
Those whose nature is too slow
Cannot satisfy a lover,
By a few strokes of the rod applied robustly,
You are able to fight more vigorously.
Let yourself easily forget a moment of suffering!
I will experience it, myself.
Take this punishment. Come on, my dear child,
Spank me wildly.
(*She gives her the whip and picks up her skirts.*)
Marton. What a ridiculous desire!

Me—I'll hit my friend!
On this body so white and so soft
Would I shower a thousand strokes?
No, no, my heart is too sensitive.
Come on now, I still feel the painful impression
Of that terrible instrument.
Agatha. I'm not kidding. Hit me, hit me, Marton.
(*Marton whips her.*)
Very good—again—harder.
Marton. Already on your thin skin
I see a beautiful vermilion arising.
Agatha. Imitate Angelica and Justine as best you can.
Be firm, hit hard until the end:
Agatha's courage is above all else.
Marton. (*Still whipping her.*) Very well, my dear. Are you satisfied?
Agatha. (*Stopping her.*) That's enough. Come, Marton, into the arms of a lover.
Let's throw ourselves on this bed: in the bosom of pleasure
Let us lose the memory of our past torments. (*They kiss each other.*)
Marton. Ah! My queen—ah! your finger—I'm dying—I'm swooning.
Agatha. Soon! soon! ah! my dear soul!
Marton. How well you know, you rascal, how to soften my pain;
What a skillful comforter! (*They get off the bed.*)
Agatha. This night, by a thousand darts of flame,
Clitandre will better prove his passion to you.
Marton. May the Jesuit equal his valor!
Agatha. Prepare a snack
To revive their exhausted vigor.
Marton. I had anticipated you;
I have ample provision of fruit and cakes;
Here is an exquisite wine.
Agatha. Ah! little trickster!

With such a charming disposition, would one believe to see her,
That tonight is her first attempt?
This foresight charms me.
Marton. I will admit, however, this first attempt alarms me.
I cannot think, without shuddering,
About the violent assaults that I will endure.
Agatha. Fie, then! no human weakness;
Do you know, looking at me,
That I can easily topple
Four Franciscan monks at the same time?
Marton. Four! Is it possible? ah! my queen,
Tell me about your gallant exploits.
Agatha. The story is a bit ticklish.
Let's suspend it for a moment. I'll go see right now
If no one's listening to us:
Every nun, they say, is nasty and curious.
Marton. Run, and come back soon to satisfy my desires.
(*Sister Agatha exits.*)
How much common sense she has at her age!
She knows how to combine, in a rare blend,
Prudence with pleasure;
Alternately, she is wise and profligate;
On her forehead, modesty serves as a veil for love:
Agatha, vestal virgin by day,
Tonight will be Messalina.
Agatha. (*Returning.*) Everyone is sleeping in the house.
I can safely satisfy your curiosity now.
I was not yet fifteen,
When the flame that devours us
Started to burst in my restless heart.
A voluptuous intoxication
Seized my senses in the arms of sleep,

And I knew with skill
How to extend it when awake.
My mother, a zealous devotee,
Brought me every month to confess in detail;
To Father Adrien, every time
I went to tell my story.
Marton. Ah! I know this son of Saint Francois very well,
To whom had you been entrusted!
T— rang out with his gallant exploits.
Agatha. He listened eagerly
To the confession of tender weaknesses.
Curious about the details, he skillfully knew
How to encourage me with his caresses,
To speak to him sincerely.
Attracted by my charms, by my naivete,
And by my warm temperament,
He calmed the remorse of my fearful soul
And created in my heart a violent desire
To see myself in the fellowship
Of the order of the great Saint Francis.
The day was chosen for the ceremony:
It was the day after Twelfth Night.
Dressed like a bride,
Alone, and early in the morning, I go to the convent;
My young heart is beating, and my smoldering soul
Seems to foresee the happiness that awaits it.
The charitable father immediately places me
In a secret chapel;
He locks the door, to keep out the noise
And any indiscreet encounter.
"My dear child," he says, "by your determination
You must make yourself worthy

To receive the distinguished honor
That Saint Francis reserves for your piety.
A useful correction
From his seraphic belt
Before being in possession,
Must punish this unclean flesh,
The source of temptation.
My hand will begin this beneficial work;
Won't you, my dear,
Through a few moments of pain
Ensure your eternal happiness today?"
I consent to everything with joy.
The rascal kisses me: he unfolds
His long whip. Enslaved to his blows,
To the laws he prescribes for me I obey without a sound;
Body naked to the waist,
I bow down to his knees:
On my back immediately I feel the storm falling;
I support it with courage.
At the end he stops, and full of emotion:
"That's enough; in the womb of this pure virgin,
Let us place," he says, "the holy cord."
He forbids me to change my posture
And urges me to suffer with devotion
The pious operation.
Marton. I admire the imposture of these cockroach monks.
Ah! How I fear for you the painful introduction
Of the terrible cord.
But continue your story.
Agatha. I felt pierced
By a large peg inserted with force.
I suffered everything without batting an eyelid:

A violent shock,

With stinging pain

The whole spike entered.

At the same time the pain ceases;

I experience an amorous intoxication,

And by the lively tremors

Of the holy director who presses me

I second the movements.

Soon, through torrents of flame,

It floods, it penetrates, it sets my soul ablaze;

I breathe; Adrien redoubles his efforts.

Hardly made for such transports,

I burn, I shiver, I fall—I faint.

Marton. Stop, Agatha, spare me;

Right now, I'm as weak as you are.

Agatha. Restored by these cares from this enchanting disorder,

I grab hold of myself greedily.

I devoutly kiss

A rope with large knots that he shows me.

The director smiles, and feeling reborn,

Kisses me affectionately:

"So that the tempter does not dare to reappear,

My daughter, we need another application

Of the holy cord."

"Ah!" I say, "right now, my father,

I feel more than ever that I need it."

I bow down and instantly tuck up my skirts.

In his conquest, he returns as a conqueror,

And roams with an easy gait

Through the road ablaze with pleasure.

I stir voluptuously beneath him,

The lover's liquor is dripping in a moment—

Marton. In good faith, tell me, my dear,
Didn't you suspect anything about this gallant mystery?
Agatha. I suspected it at first, but for good reasons,
I thought I had to hide my joy and my suspicions.
Tired of such constraint,
The second time, I repressed all pretense;
I turned my head, and without further ado,
Reaching for the blessed father's collar,
I grabbed his cord, still hot and steaming,
Which, limp and without vigor, hung languidly.
Caught in the act, the monk was sincere.
He confessed to me
That more than one stern devotee
Does as much, every day,
And that the holy cord, applied frequently,
Kept the monastery busy.
Marton. This is how, by abusing religion,
It is used to hide their infamous practices.
Should we be surprised if women
Have so much affection for the sons of Francis!
Agatha. How I love your devotion!
Let's continue. He wanted to enter the quarry,
I obey; but unfortunately! the strength of the good father
Responds badly to his desires.
Touched by my burning sighs:
"I am going," he says, "to the monastery.
To look for some friends; it's in their arms, my dear,
That you'll to taste robust pleasures."
He goes out, and soon he brings in
Three vigorous young monks.
No sooner had they arrived
Than I feel pressed into their anxious arms.

Instantly, against me each spike is erected;
They attack me at the same time.
"Ah! Heavens!" I cried frightened.
"How will I resist such fighters?"
Marton. Your fate makes me tremble. How, my dear Agatha,
Both so young and so delicate,
Could she support the furious assaults
Of four fiery satyrs?
No, I can't understand it.
Agatha. You will hear how I managed them.
To avoid any rivalry,
The order among them was determined by lot.
Father Andre was happy: trussing up skirt and shirt,
On the edge of an old bench he arranges me as he pleases,
And penetrating quickly,
Loving nectar engulfs me in a moment.
Father Ambroise immediately rushes over to me;
A moment is enough for him. Father Roch came next.
My daughter, I must confess,
To the glory of the latter,
If he looks like the least brilliant of the four,
He has a vigor that nothing can destroy.
How really funny was my fate!
Three times, without restraining, he inserted his cock.
He was about to begin a new pursuit,
When, jealous of his rights, the fuming director,
Snatching him furiously from my arms,
In spite of me, seized the citadel.
Marton. Agatha, now I no longer fear for you.
Heavens! What ecstasies! What delights!
The mere telling sirs me. I'm beside myself.
Agatha. Each on my altar offered five sacrifices.

We had to leave each other. Consider my sorrow!
I felt an extreme heat under my skirt, a cruel itch;
I was ready to begin again more beautifully,
If their vigor had been able
To respond to my passion.
Marton. I admire your proud valor:
What a pity, my dear, being of this temperament,
That you are enclosed in this lonely place,
To dispense reluctantly
Involuntary wisdom!
Agatha. Don't arouse my grief;
Marton, I know what it costs me.
Marton. This brilliant and sweet trial,
No doubt, my dear, pledges you
To see your director often?
Agatha. In the grip of his vibrant tenderness,
I used to spend two hours with him every day;
I was in the arms of love,
When I was believed to have been in confession.
My mother, admiring my fervor,
Allowed me full freedom,
But a cruel reverse came to disturb my happiness.
Unfortunately, I had a brother;
He wanted to enrich himself at his sister's expense;
I was put in the convent. The caressing nuns
Enchanted me with their sweet, seductive way of life.
Alas! I was still ignorant of the charms of the world;
My mother was pressing me, I did not resist;
I let myself be bound by a bitter chain,
Which soon forever—but the bell is calling me;
Someone surely brings me
News from my lover.

Marton. Ah! My impatience is equal to yours.
I follow in your footsteps, my queen.
My heart is beating. God of pleasures,
Fulfill a shy girl's desires.

End of Act Two.

Act Three

Agatha. Everything follows according to plan,
Marton, a young child was waiting for me at the door;
Our lovers sent him; come quickly, I bring you
The answers of both.
How tenderly I will caress my Jesuit!
See the letter he's written to me. (*She reads.*)
"I will pay homage to your charms tonight,
We will make Marton forget her disgrace.
Receive Priapus in your arms
Under the mantle of Saint Ignatius."
Marton. If the father's vigor equals his spirit,
How happy your fate is, my dear.
Let's see what Clitandre writes. (*She reads.*)
"Tonight, in the shadow of mystery,
Marton, I fly to your knees.
I swear by the god of Love, I swear by his mother,
Your fortunate lover will be worthy of you."
This post is lovely.
Agatha. Each has its merit.
If Clitandre's message is more respectful,
I see in the Jesuit's
A livelier, more familiar, more loving tone.
Marton. Should we be surprised? Until now,
My wisdom had taught me how to defend myself
Against Clitandre's enthusiasm.
The master of your charms, the father, is less flattering
Of a commodity that he has already sampled.
But, hush—I hear some noise—ah! how emotional I am!
They're entering—Where can I hide? Ah, heaven! I'm lost.
(*Enter Clitandre and the Jesuit.*)

Jesuit. (*Thrusting himself at Agatha's neck.*)

My queen, I fly to your voice.

That by this kiss full of flame,

Repeated a thousand and a thousand times,

All my fires pass into your soul!

Clitandre. (*At Marton's knees.*)

You're avoiding me, Marton; ah! what cruelty!

Yield to the desires of your most tender lover.

Stop defending yourself from my emotions,

In these happy moments made for voluptuousness.

Marton. (*Struggling.*)

Into what abyss, Agatha, oh, heavens! have you led me!

Agatha. What! You're behaving like a child? You're pretending to resist?

Don't hesitate to give in to pleasure. (*She kisses her.*)

Come, shy Marton; my heart congratulates you

For the happiness you will savor.

Jesuit. (*Dragging Agatha away.*) That's enough; let's leave them, my dear:

Your presence is not necessary

To bring together these two lovers.

Let's not waste precious moments in this way.

Agatha. How could I be unyielding?

Let's go to this nearby sofa,

With a torrent of pleasure coming to flood my breast;

I surrender to you, my dear father.

(*They retire to the back of the stage, and kiss.*)

Marton. (*While Clitandre knocks her down on the bed and pulls up her skirts.*)

Ah! Clitandre, what are you doing?

What! Are you undressing me?

Clitandre. Allow me to worship on my knees

The celestial attractions with which Love has provided you—

Let me contemplate the whiteness of your body,

The elasticity, the freshness.

Forgive an amorous whim;
With this ardent kiss I take possession
Of this little place of delights,
Shaded by a thick fleece.
Marton. (*Stiring.*) What are you thinking? Stop, Clitandre.
Clitandre. (*Throwing himself on her.*)
Banish a ridiculous fright.
Marton. You're throwing yourself on top of me!
Cruel man, from your raptures I cannot defend myself.
At least let me, dear lover,
Position myself more conveniently.
(*She adjusts herself and crosses her legs over Clitandre's back.*)
Agatha. (*Coming closer.*)
Well! Friend, is Marton still a virgin?
Clitandre. I've finally tamed this rebellious beauty.
I'm going to light a fire
In this charming little den.
Agatha. Don't spare her.
Marton. Ah! cruel man! what a martyrdom!
What a size!—he's tearing me apart—
Stop—phew!—he's killing me—stop for just a moment—
The executioner is still going; he doesn't want to hear me.
Jesuit. Be insensitive to his torment:
It is not the occasion to be tender.
Marton. He's becoming twice as hard—the dog—ah! ah!
Clitandre. I am victorious—
To calm your pain, I'm going to
Pour a healthy cream on your wound;
Do you feel it? Do you feel it, my dear?
Marton. (*Shaking.*) I feel a sweet heat
Which penetrates me to the heart.
I can feel the distillation drop by drop—

Pierce—plunge, lovable conqueror,

Don't mess around on the way—

Push, friend—push hard—

Where am I? I'm dying—support me, dear lover—

Clitandre. (*Getting up.*) Will my queen forgive me?

I can imagine what she must have suffered.

For young beauty, cruel necessity

Requires that pleasure be obtained through pain.

Marton. (*Lowering her petticoats.*)

Joy and regret struggle in turn,

I hardly dare to look at you, cruel man.

Goodbye virtue, wisdom, honor,

A moment has soiled my glory and my modesty!

Dear Clitandre, ha! at least if you were faithful to me!

You attack, you subjugate, you forget a beauty?

Clitandre. (*Tenderly.*) Banish these odious suspicions.

Gratified by your favors, I will love you more;

Come: I want to seal the promise on your body.

Marton. (*Leading Clitandre.*) Very well! enjoy my frailty—

Get on that bed with me.

I surrender all to you.

Jesuit. (*To Sister Agatha.*) Will they alone accomplish the loving sacrifice?

Relieve my torment—deign, amiable novice,

To offer me, against the grain, the object of my desires.

Any road can lead to the temple of pleasures.

Agatha. Ah! what a tyrannical lover!

You want it, you have to earn it.

(*She sits up and raises her skirts; the Jesuit bends over her and threatens a false attack.*)

No Jesuitical kiss, rogue,

Or forever I'll give up seeing you.

I do not claim to receive you

Only in the canonical way.
Jesuit. Beautiful Agatha, you know your power over me—
I won't hurt you.
If sometimes in college, we gave such lessons
To our young boys,
It was to relieve nature.
Get up, my sister.
Am I okay?
Agatha. Push, vigorously—
Push, friend; don't be afraid to rattle your mount.
Jesuit. How you gobbled it up! As the prize for your ardor,
Receive this fiery dart.
Agatha. What a subtle flame
Distills in my burning heart—
Won't you finish—I can't stand it—
I'm about to die from pleasure.
Marton. (*Pulling the Jesuit by his robe.*)
Come on, libertine, give me back my friend.
Athletes, suspend your thrusts.
I bring cakes for Clitandre and for you;
This wine will rekindle your dying flame.
Let's drink! Let us pay tribute in turn
To Bacchus! To Eros!
(*They eat and drink. Meanwhile Agatha and Clitandre slip away.*)
Marton. Father, where is your mistress going?
Clitandre followed in her footsteps,
They left us alone; didn't they count
A little too much on our discretion?
Jesuit. (*Kissing Marton*) Clitandre has taken away my property—
I'll take revenge on his beauty.
Marton. (*Smiling.*) Let's punish this unfaithful couple—
I won't deny you anything

Jesuit. (*Running his hand under Marton's skirt.*)
Let my hand take hold
Of the treasure that is delivered to my flames.
Allow it, Marton, to get lost
In the labyrinth of love.
(*He positions Marton's hand.*)
Seize the goods that miserly nature
Intended for you to enrich me—
Beneath your fingers watch them grow.
Priapus, on fire, seeks an asylum:
Deign to receive it.
Marton. I cannot consent to it.
Eh! Who could please him?
Jesuit. The less easy the journey,
The more pleasurable it will be.
(*He draws Marton to him.*)
Hasten to pierce yourself with my shaft.
Quickly—quickly—
Marton. (*On the knees of the Jesuit, shaking vigorously.*)
Ah! my king! do you perceive how I love you?
Agatha. (*Seeing Marton, astride the Father.*)
Ah! ah! ah! what a funny contraption!
Running like that, kind post-horse,
You'll soon arrive at the inn.
Jesuit. My nun, it suits you to speak in this tone:
I'm taking revenge for your flight.
Marton. I'm being unfaithful to you, dear Clitandre—
Should I have been left alone with a Jesuit?
Clitandre. Go, go on, you deserve it.
Let's each forget our abuse,
And to awaken our desires,
With a new attitude,

Let's diversify our pleasures.
Let us leave this vain finery
And these odious clothes—
Lovers are never better
Than in a purely natural state. (*They undress.*)
Jesuit. (*Undoing Marton's corset.*)
Come, lovely child, unveil without qualms
This charming body, worthy of the gods.
Clitandre. (*Uncovering Sister Agatha's breast.*)
Under this ridiculous wimple,
Ah! my sister, what charms you hide from our eyes!
May everyone listen to me in silence:
Agatha will be so kind
As to lie down on this sofa.
The Father will grab her.
On the back of Her Reverence,
Immediately, Marton will stretch out:
I'll open the dance with her.
With each blow received, my beauty
Will fall back on the Father.
With this help, his slender sword
Will enter the nun even harder—
When, thrust toward the Jesuit
Agatha will rise up—
Marton, pushed by the Father,
Will go before my thrusts.
Let's put this project into practice.
(*They arrange themselves.*)
Let each apply himself to his role.
This voluptuous ricochet
Will make all four of us happy.
Agatha. Stop. I'm crushed.

Jesuit. Oh! You won't escape me.

Marton. Dear Clitandre, double down.

Agatha. Ah! What abundant dew

Floods my secret charms!

Marton. I taste supreme delight!

Clitandre. And me! Marton.

Jesuit. Same goes for me.

(*After a moment of silence, they separate.*)

Agatha. Let's go to rest. Let's sing in unison:

Long live the author of this creation!

Dear friends, let's drink to his glory

What! Marton, don't you dare to drink?

Do you need to swallow the amorous nectar

In large drafts to calm your fires?

(*They drink and eat.*)

Clitandre. Marton, my fire is reborn. Turn around, my dear—

Give me that charming back

That two veiled monkeys, not long ago,

Have treated so cruelly.

(*He turns her over.*)

Ah! heavens! I recognize the trace of whip lashes.

With less annoying blows I must erase it.

Come on, rump high and head low

Stand firm, and above all don't reject me.

(*He gets on top of her.*)

Marton. (*Struggling.*)

What are you doing, villain? Ah, heavens! what infamy!

Come to my aid, dear friend—

He's deviating from the right path

To penetrate next door.

Agatha. Clitandre, beware of offending the nature

Of this lovable object, by an impure flame.

Do not profane her attractions.
(*She pulls him off from Marton, who goes out.*)
Clitandre. (*Running after Agatha.*)
Okay, but you will pay the cost.
(*He knocks her down and kisses her.*)
Agatha. (*Kissing Clitandre.*)
I approve of your revenge. In honor of a friend
I see that I must sacrifice myself.
Jesuit. (*Attacking Clitandre from behind.*)
What! while you fuck each other,
You think that I would stay with folded arms!
Forgive my robe, Clitandre;
Seeing the plumpness and the vivid whiteness
Of your pretty behind,
I could not defend myself from an Italian taste.
Continue, don't disturb yourself—
If necessary, to affect you, I'll double the pace.
Clitandre. (*After they have finished.*)
I excuse you, father, for the anti-physical taste:
It comes from a Jesuitical habit.
But when the vows can be fulfilled with agreeable sex,
How can one cherish this shameful trade!
Jesuit. This taste is not so ridiculous—
Hylas was the darling of Hercules;
Socrates, we are told, burned
For Alcibiades and Phaedon—
Jupiter, in love, kidnapped Ganymede—
Hyacinthe amused the leisure hours of Apollo—
Caesar stroked Nicomedes—
In Rome, the queen of nations,
Every emperor had his boys.
Those who lived in Greece and Italy, at all times,

Followed this sweet obsession—
Even today, with success,
It reigns among the French.
Agatha. Keep quiet, seducer! Such infamy
Can only excite my wrath.
It owes its birth to that unholy sect
Who would want to do without us.
To burn with ardor both reciprocal and pure,
Man and woman were created;
To prostitute one's sex, to insult nature,
In my eyes, has always been the greatest of crimes.
Marton. (*Leaving the room where she had taken refuge.*)
I bring sad news:
Friends, with the night our pleasures will end.
Agatha, the bell is calling you,
And the sky is beginning to turn white.
Agatha. Farewell then, vigorous athletes,
Objects of our burning desires.
From time to time, bring back to these sad retreats
Love, games and pleasures.
While twenty easy beauties, Clitandre,
Will yield, in turn, to your ecstasies—
And docile schoolgirls, dear Father,
Will, every day, provide for your needs—
Between these thick walls forever tightened,
I will see, in tears, my days being consumed,
If, touched by the torments of a lost girl,
You don't come to revive them.
Jesuit. No, I will not receive such a fatal farewell.
Beautiful ladies, we only have one moment left,
To celebrate anew your charms.
Let us resume our tender frolics.

Marton. Before we begin again,
Reassure our delicate hearts—
Dear friends, do not deceive us.
Swear that at the slightest notice,
Full of faithful ardor, you will fly to our arms.
Clitandre, Jesuit. We both swear.
Clitandre. May the god of Kythera
Make us feel his anger,
If you burn for ungrateful lovers!
But let's take advantage of the time. Marton, be less serious—
The moment your young lover
Will enter the temple of pleasures from the front,
Open the other door to the good Father—
While your libertine finger
Is foraging the charms of the dashing sister,
The lovely nun, with a playful tickle,
Will hasten the effect of our weapons.
Jesuit. Dear Clitandre, why do you delay?
From her cave, Venus grants you entry—
Marton, receive without wrath
This burning dart, whose thrusts
Ignite new fires in your intoxicated soul.
Let us thrust—let us thrust in unison
Inside the voluptuous Marton;
Let us redouble her tender delirium;
May her senses be unable to cope with
The impetuous passion of our desires—
Let us make her succumb under the weight of pleasure.
Clitandre, May your tickling, Agatha,
Increase my felicity!
Agatha. Marton, may your delicate hand,
By its frolicsome activity,

Scatter voluptuousness through my agitated senses!
Marton. Quickly—dear friend—I'm dying—I'm fainting—
With delicious cloudbursts
Appease the passion that ignites me—
I feel—ah! what pleasure! you both flooded me.
Agatha. Stop, Marton, I wouldn't know how to cope with
Such a sweet thrill!
Marton. What impetuous thrusts!
Clitandre. A voluptuous tremor!
Jesuit. Sweet languor—fiery delirium!
We tasted the ecstasy of the gods.
(*They fall onto the sofa.*)
Clitandre. Pick up our clothes. Farewell, lovely girls,
Whose kind naivete
Erases the attractions of those cold lovers
Guided either by whim or greed.
Beautiful without art and adornment,
Tender with sincerity,
You know how to brighten up an austere enclosure,
And you follow in freedom
The sweet inclination of nature.
How I regret leaving this enchanting sojourn!
In the world, love is harsh slavery—
Feelings and language,
Everything breathes fraud and infidelity—
A woman's modesty is a hypocritical mask.
Falsehood reigns in its sweetest emotions—
It is in the cloister alone
Where real voluptuousness lives.

The End.

The Intrigue at the Brothel
(1830)
Vaudeville in one Act
by
M. D.

The Intrigue at the Brothel *was printed for the first time in an edition of* Le Théâtre gaillard *published at the latest during the last years of the Bourbon Restoration, probably in 1830, under the rubric of London, Alfeston and Co. This vaudeville, attributed, perhaps wrongly, to Marc-Antoine Madeleine Désaugiers (1772–1827) seems to date from the First Empire. Educated at the Mazarin College in Paris, Désaugiers emigrated to the French colony of Santo Domingo during the French Revolution; but following the rebellion in that country (begun in August 1791), he moved to the United States, where he gave piano lessons to scrape together a living wage. He returned to France in 1797 where he became a popular playwright of light comedies, operas, and vaudevilles and a successful theatre manager at the Vaudeville from 1815 to 1820. While out of character with his dramatic work,* The Intrigue at the Brothel *does exhibit many of the idiosyncracies of Désaugiers's satiric songs, and for that reason, the erotic vaudeville was attributed to him.*

Characters

Mother Bishop, madam
Flora, premiere courtesan
Justine,
Leonore,
Josephine, prostitutes
Victoria, a probationer
Saint-Elme, a wily young officer
Godichon, son of Rooster-Leg, coming from the country
Rooster-Leg, invalid corporal
M. Duguichet, a police informer
Prostitutes
Pimps
Tricks
A patrol

(*The action takes place at the Palais Royal, number 113.*)

Flora. (*She walks in humming the tune, "In the shade of an old oak tree."*)
My father's balls
Are hanging to the floor,
My mother is desperate
To see them dry up. (*She pauses.*)

What, nobody here? Where is that slut Justine, that bitch Eleonore—I don't know what they're up to; for public women they are hardly organized—(*She continues her tune.*)

Sometimes she presses them
To get the juice out,
And rubs her buttocks with them,
And her asshole.

Mother Bishop. (*Entering.*) Sing, sing, hussy. I'll bring you down to earth.

Flora. It's you, mother. What's the matter?

Mother Bishop. It's that I've—the sacred name of fucking!—it's that I've—I'm awfully mad.

Flora. Why?

Mother Bishop. Why?—I'm dishonored! It's eleven o'clock, the gallery full of men: officers, senators, foreigners, and not a trick!—bitches that you are, you get fucked for a hundred louis of gold and diamonds up your ass—not a trick!—and I, who had my large living room repainted with gilding, antique borders, in the most modern taste—and not a trick.

Flora. Don't be mad, mother.

Mother Bishop. A thousand thunderclaps! I'm not angry, but fuck! Is it worth it to throw yourself into hellish expenses when commerce is dead, when men no longer pay, when it is necessary to pay the government a thousand ecus for a license, to the landlord, a thousand ecus for rent, and then the surgeons, the doctors, dressmakers, fashion vendors, hairdressers, and above all that, hags like you, who don't even earn what the skin of your ass is worth, who eat and drink like dykes, and who stay all day, arms crossed and legs dangling, scratching your twat—a great profit! (*Sings, to the tune, "We'll get married tomorrow."*)

On Monday, I bought
Very pretty corset:
Rose tears its sleeve;
On Tuesday, a pinafore
Filled with poop;
From a kick to the hip,
She soiled her pleated dress,
So white—
All is finished,
I am here
Very frank:
If Saturday,
Is like today,
I won't give a fuck about anything on Sunday.

Flora. Hey! No, mother. Everything will work out. (*She sings, to the tune, "Hey! Mother, do I know that."*)

If fate too severe
Overwhelms you with its setbacks,
We will weaken it, I hope
By working better for you.
Yes, we will shake our buttocks
With a new zeal:
Make us fuck endlessly,
Instead of your giving the fuck up.

(*Enter Justine, Leonore, and Josephine, who reprise the refrain in chorus.*)

Make us fuck endlessly,
Instead of your giving the fuck up.

Mother Bishop. (*Ironically.*) Here is a well-equipped whorehouse! Where are you coming from so cheerfully?

Josephine. Myself—I've just made men; here are two louis; I mounted two soldiers and my big English banker; he regaled me with his boxing ability—Oh! He's a good kid: long live the bankers! (*Sings, to the tune "I've seen everywhere in my travels."*)

I prefer this breed;
Should I tell the reason?
They never make a face,
And their money is flowing in abundance.
They are our only resources;
With us, in urgent need,
By scratching their wallets a little,
We make their money tumble down.

Leonore. I wasn't so lucky. I had to deal with an old prosecutor: I did all I could, but he was too hard-hearted and his prick too soft. Nevertheless, he had brought rods so he could be whipped; I dislocated my wrist, and the animal was no harder than a comet. (*Sings, to the tune "From top to bottom."*)

From top to bottom

I was crushing his ugly behind;
From top to bottom
I hit him with all my strength;
His prick, colder than a prick made of stone,
Hung like a beer sign,
From top to bottom.

(*Spoken.*) Tired of finally tearing up his carcass, I asked him for his present, as is the practice. Didn't he just turn a deaf ear, claiming that I had to get him hard, and then he would pay me—that was the *sine qua non*. I told him that I couldn't understand Latin, and I called Francis. (*Sings, to the tune "Jump through the crossroads."*)

"Will you let go of your ecu!"
Francis said to him in anger,
"If not, old ass-mold,
I'll work you over my way."
The other responds: "Fuck yourself!"
Francis, who doesn't understand scorn,
Grabs him, and on the spot,
Makes him jump through the window.

(*Spoken.*) He left me only an old hat, and a pendant, which Francis grabbed.

Mother Bishop. So be it! Now that! You others, at work, and especially so that no one makes me a doormat, I don't harken to that. (*Sings to the tune " Monsieur Mulard, or, In hell, as when traveling."*)

In the brothel as well as in business,
Never give credit;
Let Eros, at the temple of Kythera,
Sell his favors at all costs.
To celebrate our sweet mysteries,
Pay, gentlemen, pay us straightforward;
Our favors will be dearer to you
When you have bought our love.

(*The ensemble sings.*)

In the brothel as well as in business,
Never give credit;
Let Eros, at the temple of Kythera,
Sell his favors at all costs.
To celebrate our sweet mysteries,
Pay, gentlemen, pay us straightforward;
Our favors will be dearer to you
When you have bought our love.

(*All the girls exit.*)

Mother Bishop. (*Alone.*) Let someone say after that that I'm not wrong. Oh! we madams earn money only by the sweat of our bodies. It's true that I can boast of practicing with honor. Whitewashed in cum—thirty-six years in the business! To how many people, as well, have I not been useful! What service have I not rendered to humanity! (*Sings, to the tune "I lost my ass."*)

In every street
Girls are lost.
I come to their aid,
And I always find
Lost girls.

(*Spoken.*) Little Victoria, for example, whom I met yesterday on Tire-Boudin Street, was fleeing from her paternal home; her mother was being too strict with her. I saw her worn-looking face, her stature, her breast, and I adopted her; in addition, how cruel can a mother be, to want to lock up her daughter, a fifteen-year-old embroiderer! (*Sings, to the tune "I will always understand you well."*)

Ladies, why use locks
To guard the honor of your daughters?
Doesn't Eros know how, without you,
To slip through the gates?
Despite the care of their mothers,
How many nice embroiderers,
More than once, have had their needles
Threaded by their lovers.

Saint-Elme. (*He enters, laughing out loud.*) Ha! ha! ha! How precious! Ha! ha!

Mother Bishop. Why the gaiety?

Saint-Elme. He couldn't be nicer! Ha! Ha!

Mother Bishop. Who are you talking about?

Saint-Elme. A fool I just fooled. Ha! Ha!

Mother Bishop. Oh! my good man. You have to explain that to me.

Saint-Elme. Exceptional. Ha! Ha!

Mother Bishop. Then again, tell me what's going on.

Saint-Elme. So, imagine a very lean individual, very tall, of pleasant appearance, mottled stockings, wide tie, canary coat with ribbing, and sugar loaf hat, a stick in his hand—

Mother Bishop. What a description!

Saint-Elme. This gracious character, freshly descended from the Auxerre coach, and for whom I have just dismounted at the Cafe Borel—

Mother Bishop. I guess the rest.

Saint-Elme. One moment, what you haven't guessed is that I relocated said individual to your brothel.

Mother Bishop. Nice customer! and what do you want me to do with him?

Saint-Elme. At your discretion. Besides, you can rest easy, I'm paying for him.

Mother Bishop. So be it!

Saint-Elme. You can imagine, however, that for my money I want to enjoy myself; the simpleton is relying on me to present him to the world and to launch him in good society. In response to his confidence, I'm introducing him to the brothel. Without his father's knowledge, he came to spend his holidays in Paris, and I'm taking him to these places. You are a widow of station, you live on your own, you have grown-up daughters to marry, your hotel is the meeting place for the important people in the capital: behave accordingly.

Mother Bishop. Oh! That's a lot of crap!

Saint-Elme. Fuck! With such words, farewell to the woman of quality!

Mother Bishop. Anyway, I don't give a fuck. I will try to speak properly; so, we were saying?

Saint-Elme. That you should treat my friend like a very wealthy young man—

Mother Bishop. Very well.

Saint-Elme. To whom one of your sluts, under the name of the lady of the house, will lavish the sweetest favors.

Mother Bishop. Justine—accommodatingly adept, with six months' experience.

Saint-Elme. Excellent. You've got the right idea.

Mother Bishop. He wants to make his entry into the world, oh! How I will advance him! Listen. (*Sings, to the tune "Childish," from the vaudeville, the* Knife-grinder and the Miller.)

We will start the work,

By giving him a whore,

This is the wisest way

To get him started nicely.

Saint-Elme. Marvelous! (*Sings.*)

To complete his gear,

We can present him

With syphilis for his journey—

Mother Bishop. All right, if he's under my care,

The pox is his share.

We will run it well!

What a delight!

Then suddenly

The clap,

Swollen glands,

Malignant tumors,

Benign skin lesions,

Will finally lead him

To the Capuchins.

Do you see the crew from here:

Cankers, pox and whore?

Yes, by these means, I pledge

That he will make his way.

Saint-Elme. Oh! The pleasant crew,

Cankers, pox and whore!

Yes, the means are very wise

For him to make his way.

Saint-Elme. (*Spoken.*) You're really charming. I have to kiss you.

Mother Bishop. Are you crazy? Let me go, I think I hear someone. Ah! Good lord, that's your bitch, no doubt.

Godichon. (*Entering.*) The scoundrel, what impudence! To dare to play me like that!

(*He sees Mother Bishop and bows deeply.*)

Saint-Elme. Allow me, madam, to introduce you to the young man who—

Godichon. (*Bowing again.*) Yes, madam, I'm the young man who—

Saint-Elme. Who has just experienced the saddest escapade.

Godichon. A bad trick, and for which I would take revenge if I dared.

Mother Bishop. So, what is this adventure? I deserve to be informed of it, sir; please—

Godichon. Madam, in truth—

Mother Bishop. I beg you.

Godichon. Certainly—

Saint-Elme. Hey! Why all the fuss? Come to the point.

Godichon. It's fitting to tell you that I was in this cafe that we found—

Saint-Elme. We know that. Continue—

Godichon. (*Sings, to the tune "Monsignor d'Orleans."*)

Now, here is the case;

Don't interrupt me,

You'll see

What was my despair;

I hear myself clearly being called,

I get up and hear nothing,
I sit down again; immediately
Someone's calling me, and I remain a fool.
Have I lost my head,
Do people take me for a simpleton?
"Monsieur Godichon!"
Of course! that's my name.
I suddenly answer: "Who is calling me?
—Mr. Godichon!
—Well! what do you want from me?
—Quickly, to the staircase:
Your uncle from Dijon
Is bringing you a turkey.
—It's good."
I get up and run. I wait,
I ask all passers-by;
Three times I go up and down,
All ready to lose common sense.
Finally, the cafe owner,
Seeing my blood heat up,
Tells me, "That's enough, my boy."
I recognize the voice!
It was my uncle from Dijon,
And I was the turkey!

Flora. (*Rushing in.*) What's so amusing?
Mother Bishop. Go fuck yourself!
Godichon. (*Quietly to Saint-Elme.*) Who is that charming person?
Saint-Elme. (*In confidence.*) One of the daughters of the house.
Flora. But come on; they can't enjoy Victoria, she doesn't want to work.
Saint-Elme. Who is this Victoria?
Mother Bishop. (*Softly, in his ear.*) A little bitch. (*Aloud.*) A parent. (*Softly.*) A virgin for sale.

Saint-Elme. Really!—I would be delighted to make her acquaintance.

(*He places two louis in Mother Bishop's hand.*)

Mother Bishop. You win. Sir, I'll give her the honor. The duties of my home are calling me, but I'm not saying goodbye to you.

Saint-Elme. (*Softly.*) Don't forget the pox.

Mother Bishop. (*Softly.*) I'll put her aside, in this closet. (*Aloud.*) Gentlemen, adieu.

Saint-Elme. All the best. (*Mother Bishop and Flora exit.*)

Godichon. She couldn't be nicer.

Saint-Elme. And the young lady?

Godichon. Ravishing. Oh, my friend. What an acquaintance!

Saint-Elme. You can't imagine how much you will gain here. But, by the way, you haven't yet told me about the beauties of your district. How do you govern them?

Godichon. You mean how they govern me. (*Sings, to the tune "My father was a blighter."*)

To one, if I am courting;

"Finish, rude man!"

To the other, I spoke of love:

"You're a beast!"

Then it's screaming,

Scornful attitudes,

As soon as I touch them.

Saint-Elme. Stupid! (*Sings.*)

Brave their spite;

It is with a prick

That we shut their mouths. (*Spoken.*) So, you're still a virgin.

Godichon. Alas!

Saint-Elme. At twenty-five a big boy like you, aren't you ashamed? So, how did you occupy yourself in your village?

Godichon. (*Sings, to the tune "At daybreak."*)

At daybreak,

I jerked off, to celebrate the dawn,

With my five fingers in turn,

In the evening I expected the return.

Frequently, I still jerked off

At daybreak!

Saint-Elme. You big asshole! Let me do it, I'll train you—courses on girls, how to cop ass, to play roulette. Get started in decent society, lose your money, catch the pox, fuck me all the bitches with tight assholes, imitate me. I shake off prejudice, I don't give a damn about the censors: long live the cunt! long live the ass! (*Sings, to the tune of "I love strength in wine, or, Wine, I say, and women."*)

O you, who creates all of my happiness,

Unique object of my desire,

Sex adored, enchanting sex,

Of regret, sometimes, I sigh.

Yes, I would like, at the same time,

To provide a dual quarry at your place,

And when I fuck you from the front,

To be able to fuck you from behind.

(*Spoken.*) I'll repeat. Long live the cunt! long live the ass!

(*Sings.*) They offer me the charming image

Of the happy path of pleasure.

I gayly like to browse it

With the beauty that enchants me.

But I would see more pleasure there,

If it became, at my prayer,

A little narrower in front,

A little wider from behind.

(*Spoken.*) As for me, this is my project.

(*Sings, to the tune "of a quickened step."*)

I'll take a fifteen-year-old woman,

Sweet, kind and pretty,

And night and day I'll fuck her,

Because such is my desire.
Then when old age comes
I will be the master
Of fucking—

Godichon. (*Hearing a noise.*) What's that?

Saint-Elme. Shit! Through the window! (*We hear loud bursts of laughter in the next room, coming from the tricks.*) It seems to me that the company is gathered. Will you allow me to introduce you?

Godichon. But am I decent? Look how I'm dressed.

Saint-Elme. What! You're dressed like an angel. Let's go in.

Godichon. It's very dark in that corridor.

Saint-Elme. (*Pushing him.*) Hey! Go on, fuck!

Rooster-Leg. (*Entering with Mother Bishop.*) My little mother, how could you refuse me!

Mother Bishop. Go, you won't come in.

Rooster-Leg. Just a flick of the wrist, what does that cost you?

Mother Bishop. Go fuck yourself, I tell you.

Rooster-Leg. (*Sings, to the tune "About the stormy evening."*)

I have demonstrated in the field of honor:
At your place, I can compete.

Mother Bishop. (*Sings.*)

I don't believe in your worth
You're no longer suitable to serve.
May the State repay you,
It is up to it to pay its debts:
But, at my home,
I do not grant pensions
To the invalids.

(*Spoken.*) Come on, go around, old fellow!

Rooster-Leg. Please!

Mother Bishop. Come on, go around, I tell you. (*Leonore, rushes in.*) Another onion [dispute], I bet.

Leonore. Ah! my God! I don't know where I am; the officer who has just entered is making a horrible hullabaloo; he plucked half the hair off of poor Justine's ass.

Mother Bishop. What? Justine!

Leonore. I don't know who told him that she has the pox.

Mother Bishop. But it wasn't Justine that I gave him. When I said that there was an onion [dispute]!—My presence is necessary; as for you, old man, stay there if you want: you can be useful to us in the event of misfortune.

Rooster-Leg. (*Amorously.*) Don't you absolutely want to?

Mother Bishop. Go on, you bore me! (*Leonore and Mother Bishop exit.*)

Rooster-Leg. (*Alone.*) How annoying. (*He takes out his prick.*) I don't masturbate any more—it was well worth it to mount that bitch! (*He places his prick inside his pants.*) Rascal! do you have a human face? (*Buttoning his pants again*) Ah! my word! let's not think about it anymore. (*He draws his pipe.*) My *brûle gueule*, here is my consolation. (*Sings, to the tune "Strawberries."*)

To revive me, indeed!

Without fruit I consume myself.

To the children let's leave this game.

When we've lost our fire,

We smoke, we smoke, we smoke.

(*Sighs are heard behind the scenes.*)

(*Spoken.*) It seems to me I hear moaning.

Godichon. (*Offstage. Sings, to the tune "It's always a pleasure."*)

Ah! what torment I endure;

Should I give it up?

Victoria. (*Singing.*)

My dear, I beg you

Don't hurt me;

You pierce my belly;

Finish, it's too much suffering.

Godichon. Wait, I think it's inside.

Victoria. God! You're killing me.

Together. It's always, always pleasing.

Rooster-Leg. (*Repeating.*) It's always, always pleasing. Hey! It makes me a bit aroused; if I could see the actors—God forgive me, I'm hard again! (*He tries to look through the keyhole.*)

Godichon. (*Throwing himself into an armchair.*) Great gods! What a scratch! I'm dying! I'm dead!

Rooster-Leg. A plague on the loudmouth!

(*They both see each other with their pricks in the air.*)

Is this a dream? What—my son Godichon!

Godichon. It's my father! (*Aside.*) Oh! Shit!

Rooster-Leg. Sir, I find it astonishing—

Godichon. Father, I am very surprised—

Rooster-Leg. To find you—

Godichon. To see you—

Rooster-Leg. In this place—

Godichon. Me as well—

Rooster-Leg. So that's how you spend your vacation! What are you doing here?

Godichon. Love.

Rooster-Leg. Love!—Imbecile! (*Sings, to the tune "If Pauline is in need."*)

Beware of the tenderness

From the women you find in brothels;

Often their sweetest caress

Hides a most cruel poison.

Miserable, here you expose yourself!

Remember my lessons;

Instead of meeting roses there,

There are only pimples.

Godichon. Why didn't you tell me that sooner!

Rooster-Leg. What?

Godichon. Listen. (*Sings, to the tune "The Word."*)

Newly landed in these surroundings,

Here I met a beautiful woman.
Pleasure shone in her eyes,
I became happy in her company;
But she deceived my passion;
I thought I was well received,
And when I gave her my heart
She gave me the clap.
Rooster-Leg. The clap?
Godichon. Yes, dad, the clap.
Rooster-Leg. A million bolts out of the blue!
(*Sings, to the tune "The Fricassee."*)
This
Will not end here.
I will avenge you, on my soul;
Believe in the wrath that ignites me.
Yes,
The whore will pay for it!
Godichon. What are you going to do?
Rooster-Leg. I'm going
Directly to the barracks;
I'll get my bag, my cartridges,
My pistols!
I'll be back;
You'll know
If it's underway, when I blow my nose,
And the whore
Will get a beautiful comeuppance!
Godichon. She polluted my blood.
Rooster-Leg. Let's come right now,
Beating drum,
Flags in the wind,
My regiment!

Godichon. (*Sings*.) Yes, this is the only way.

Avenge the affront made to my balls:

Go get your patrol;

Ah! the whore

Will get a beautiful comeuppance!

Rooster-Leg. Yes, that's the way

To avenge the honor of your balls;

I come back with my patrol,

And the whore,

Will get a beautiful comeuppance!

(*He exits.*)

Godichon. (*Alone. Ironically.*) Trust your friends now!— Trust the women, the traitors! Ah! Mademoiselle Duguichet, my amiable future, what are you going to say when you see me *in statu quo*?

Saint-Elme. (*Entering, furiously.*) Whore, slut, bitch, triple fucking hell!— Where is she, that disgusting whore? Let me stick my boot in her fucking cunt!

Godichon. What's the matter? Are you crazy?

Saint-Elme. Boy, if you were in my place, would you laugh!

Godichon. Ah! My friend, if you only knew what I caught!

Saint-Elme. Good for you, if you caught someone.

Godichon. I've caught the clap, my friend.

Saint-Elme. (*Surprised.*) Could it be true? (*He laughs out loud.*) Ha! ha! give me your hand, my dear. Ha! ha! two claps together, it's too enjoyable. (*He sings, to the tune "We must go."*)

What, dear companion in adversity,

Aren't you laughing at your misfortune?

Godichon. (*Sings*.) No, this annoying pox,

I will admit, is close to my heart.

Saint-Elme. In faith! for the evil to flow away,

My dear, I can see only one way:

The hot-piss must flow.

The hot-piss flows well.

(*Enter Mother Bishop, Flora, Josephine, Leonore, Justine, girls, pimps, Rooster-Leg and his veterans.*)

Rooster-Leg. (*Sings, to the tune "Shut up, chatterboxes, about Master Adam's ankles."*)

Yes, although we are laughed at,
We have the stature
To engage in combat
As brave soldiers.
Show me, scoundrel,
The unworthy chick,
So that my cane can go
Break her arms.

Mother Bishop. (*In a vulgar tone.*) (*Sings.*)
Go, you're half-asleep,
Stretch your stumps,
Don't touch my girls
Because my men are here.
Look, my hand is impatient,
I've got to strangle you—
Move your crutches
More quickly than that.
Believe me, old ruffian,
Withdraw your patrol.

Rooster-Leg. Don't come and sing to me bitch,
Figure of infidelity!
You will see, frog,
That I have balls,
And that my patrol
Has hair on their ass.

(*To his veterans, to urge them on. Sings, to the tune "The Cossack."*)
This is too much, friends; let's break everything!
Come on, take heart,

Let's make a fuss!

No mercy, especially to whores:

In the brothel who gives a fuck!

Rooster-Leg, Saint-Elme, Godichon. (*Sing.*)

Yes, whatever the cost,

Let's deal them a mortal blow;

We have to fuck up

The whole brothel

And rout it!

Mother Bishop, her girls, and her pimps. (*Sing.*)

Hey! quickly, let's go, run everywhere,

Very good, take heart,

Make a noise;

You break it, gentlemen, you pay for it:

We'll see who gives a fuck.

Rooster-Leg, Saint-Elme, Godichon, Veterans. (*Sing.*)

This is too much, friends; let's break everything!

Come on, take heart,

Let's make a fuss!

No mercy, especially to whores:

In the brothel who gives a fuck!

Rooster-Leg. (*Alone, imitating a contradance.*)

I'm disabled,

Not very shy,

The traitor

Will pay me,

And we'll see

Which of us will win!

Rooster-Leg, Saint-Elme, Godichon, Veterans.

Yes, let it all happen,

No mercy,

Let's smash

What we can,

Then we'll see

Which of us will have the last laugh!

Tricks. (*Arriving with trousers unbuttoned.*) (*Sing.*)

What noise do we hear everywhere?

Heavens! what rage

And what a fuss!

Gentlemen, above all, silence

When we're fucking!

Mother Bishop, her girls, and **pimps.** (*Sing.*)

Hey! quickly, let's go, run everywhere,

Very good, take heart,

Make a noise;

Break it, smash it, gentlemen, you pay for it:

We'll see who gives a fuck!

Rooster-Leg, Saint-Elme, Veterans.

This is too much, friends; let's break everything!

Come on, take heart,

Let's make a fuss!

No mercy, especially to whores:

In the brothel who gives a fuck!

Duguichet. (*When he enters, the girls line up near Mother Bishop, the men take off their hats, with the exception of Saint-Elme and the tricks.*) What's all this noise about?—Mother, is this how an honest brothel should be run?

Mother Bishop. My dear Mr. Duguichet, I assure you that I am not at all responsible.

Duguichet. So how did this come about?

Mother Bishop. I'll explain it to you. The gentleman brings this other trick to my brothel: the gentleman asks me for a bitch for him, a pox for the other; it seems that there was an onion [dispute], and it was the gentleman who swallowed it—that's what happened.

Godichon. What a speech! I'm confused.

Mother Bishop. Now these two gentlemen want to make a hullabaloo, the old man is getting involved, and the old man's division comes here to do his business; you understand that this disturbs mine.

Duguichet. (*Showing his badge*.) Gentlemen, you will follow me to the clink.

All. To the clink?

Godichon. To the clink! And we're not in agreement—

Saint-Elme. Mr. Exempt, one moment, we must come to an understanding.

Duguichet. Sir, I understand nothing.

Saint-Elme. You have ears, though.

Duguichet. That may be, but you will follow me.

Saint-Elme. You lied about it!

Duguichet. (*To his patrol*.) Soldiers! Do your duty!

Saint-Elme. (*Drawing his sword*.) I'll cut the face of the first fuckwad who touches me.

Victoria. (*Entering, throwing herself at the feet of Mr. Duguichet*.) Stop!— Father, It is I who must be punished.

Duguichet. Heavens! My daughter!—My daughter, in the brothel!

All. His daughter?

Godichon. Why, it's Victoria!

Pimps, Girls, and **Tricks**. What a discovery!

Godichon. What! It's you who just gave me—

Mother Bishop. Her virginity, nitwit, since I have to tell you.

Godichon. Could it be true, my dear Victoria? (*Sings, to the tune "Steps increased."*)

Great gods! what a pleasure for my heart!
I found my beauty;
At the whorehouse,
I had the privilege
Of meeting a virgin!
She crowned my love,
My glory knows no bounds,
Because, on this day, I achieved

Victory over Victoria.

Saint-Elme. Happy bugger!

Duguichet. Get up, my daughter; I forgive you, on condition that Monsieur Godichon does you the honor of marrying you—The corporal consents, I hope.

Rooster-Leg. I agree.

Godichon. (*Tenderly.*) Ah! I had no doubt that you would ratify and seal this tender union!—Why shouldn't this recognition have taken place before a notary?

Saint-Elme. It will go there, my friend, and here is the bride's dowry, with the approval of these gentlemen.

Duguichet. (*Doffing his hat to him.*) Sir, such noble behavior touches me deeply.

Saint-Elme. Enough compliments, I don't deserve them. This wasn't what I wanted to happen to him.

Duguichet. My son-in-law, and you, my daughter, I hope you will be wiser in the future.

Godichon. Father-in-law, if I am caught here, it'll be hot for me.

Duguichet. I'm talking to you as a friend.

(*Sings, to the tune "Pegasus is a carrying horse."*)

I'm not preventing you from fucking,

That pleasure is often mine.

It's fun, no doubt,

Allowed to all good people;

But to beings of your kind,

The cunt is often fatal:

The clap is a disease that carries

Great men to the hospital.

(*The last two lines are repeated in chorus.*)

Mother Bishop. Gentlemen, I am very flattered by what is happening. If you still have weddings to perform, girls to sell, to rent or to buy, my brothel is yours. I do the contract: I have a complete assortment of ladies, and dispatch them to the counties—all at the fairest prices, and in cash.

Duguichet. Many thanks! but in the deals we make at your house, there's always too much to lose, or too much to gain.

Godichon. Oh! that no, I will no longer be so like Job to come here to seek women; I would prefer, as the saying goes:

"Remain celibate,

Just like my father did."

Vaudeville. (*To the tune, "Let's cheerfully empty our glasses."*)

Saint-Elme. (*Sings.*) I'm a valiant soldier,

The beautiful I know how to please;

In love, as in war,

Always ready for battle,

Nothing surprises me—

I fuck, I screw,

Always with passion.

Can you, for God's sake! blame my heart?

I like the cunt, it's my happiness.

If I fuck, it's for doing

Just like my father did.

Rooster-Leg. (*Sings.*) You're children,

And you can believe me,

To fuck and drink well,

Speak to me about the old days—

Yes, our ancestors,

They're our masters!

Let us bless their fate!

They fucked from night to dawn,

Always foot on the ground and dick in hand;

But we don't fuck anymore

Like our fathers did.

Godichon. (*Sings.*) I had resigned myself.

Taking my word for it,

I risked getting the pox

And I didn't gain anything.
Still a novice,
Syphillis
Waited for me in these surroundings;
But I'm off, and thanks to the gods,
If I returned, I would prefer
No longer to masturbate, to do
Just like my father did.
A prosecutor's clerk,
Who is bored with studying,
Fleeing loneliness
Seeks happiness here;
To a thrashing
We sentence him,
And quickly to the doctor.
He doesn't care, because the next day,
Here, despite cankers and sores,
He will come back to do
Like his father did.
Victoria. (*Sings.*) Although a respectable maid,
I quite like the flowers,
Sweet talk
Makes my heart beat faster.
Lively and light,
I try to please—
Faithful to my duty,
Henceforth, leaving this boudoir,
I want to flee from the power of Eros;
But I will fuck, to do
Just like my father did.
Mother Bishop. (*Sings, to the audience.*)
Ladies in your eyes

Why those ferocious looks?
Must we get huffy
Over happy conversations?
Assume the manner
Of my method,
And follow my lesson:
Don't care what people tell you;
Always have the cock in cunt;
And let's fuck without secrecy,
Like our fathers did.
Chorus. Let's fuck without secrecy,
Like our fathers did.
(*Entertainment and general orgy.*)

The End.

Part Two

Plays from *Le Théâtre Erotique de la rue de la Santé*

The Erotic Theatre of the rue de la Santé
From The Erotic Theatre of the rue de la Santé: its story *by Auguste Poulet-Malassis (1825–1878).*

If hypocrisy were not, par excellence, the theological virtue of our sad times, this Theatre, conceived according to the simple idea of Molière, *to delight decent people*, would not need any introduction. We would raise the curtain, and the show would begin, after the overture performed by the violins.

But, unfortunately! the specialists in the criminal-law mindset of our contemporaries—all magistrates trained in the sixth chamber—see matter for trial and scandal in the naivest actions, and loudly call for explanations.

These are the explanations that we will not provide them.

What we claim to write is only the pure and succinct story of the Erotic Theatre in the rue de la Santé, a bizarre, irregular, savage, excessive theatre—but where we laughed honestly, and which has had the privilege of bringing together, in the communion of gaiety, a small number of artists and vigorous men of letters.

The elegant and poetic Bohemia of the rue du Doyenne, the coterie which brought together Théophile Gautier, Gérard de Nerval, Lassailly, Arsène Houssaye, still not a millionaire, and Chassériau, and Marilhat, and so many others—who died or were buried, vaguely and indeterminately, in a university, or who simply became great poets forced to explicate the works of Adolphe d'Dennery, to earn the money necessary for the maintenance of the vices which they were able to preserve—no longer has any reason to exist. It has disappeared—with the exquisite fervor and proud initiative which made the hearts of the valiant in 1830 beat faster.

But the pervading bourgeoisie, the cafe life, the incessant need to imitate, could not completely discipline the perennial band of men of letters and artists in whom, in spite of everything, the blood of their ancestors circulates. At certain times, irritable people feel their irritations, and want, with all their might, to protest—be it between four walls and in the depths of a cellar—against the tyranny of official soirees and gatherings where painters are mixed with scholars, and poets with serious journalists.

At this time (1861), Louis Duranty had just opened, in the Tuileries garden, a puppet theater, greeted at its dawn by the acclamations of the upper and lower press, with literary puppets, who farted alexandrines, by way of powder, in the eyes of soldiers and nannies—but who soon became like the puppets of the Champs-Élysées, and had to resign themselves to playing the traditional farce of Punchinello beating his wife, and finally being carried away by the Devil.

Amédée Rolland, whose recent successes of *The Doctor's Vacation* and *The Village Usurer* had been produced, then lived in a sort of provincial town, landlocked deep in the village of Batignolles, between the fortifications and the first houses of Clichy-la-Garenne. His house had for tenants Jean Duboys, the author of *The Will* and *The Provincial Women*, Edmond Wittersheim, and Camille Weinschenck, a traveler who had returned from Japan and, because of the difficulty of his name which bends, meows, or barks, perhaps but does not speak, was simply called 4025.

Following a lunch to which Lemercier de Neuville ("Lemerdier," to his friends) was invited, the concept was introduced to apply Duranty's ideas to a free theatre, where imagination could afford itself a career, and which would serve as a pretext to bring together for a semi-monthly supper some twenty witty people, scattered throughout the twenty corners of Paris.

The project would have been a simple conversation after drinking, but for

Lemercier de Neuville, a sort of Jack-of-all-trades, capable of more things than Jack, who immediately found the means of making a reality of the idea—and on May 27, 1862, a very special audience was invited to attend the solemn inauguration of the *Erotikon Theatron*—the Erotic Theatre.

The theatre was set up in a glazed room, the antechamber of Rolland's house.

Lemercier de Neuville was, all at once, the architect, the mason, the painter, the machinist, and the director. The privilege of the directorship was, of course, solemnly granted to him.

Above the front door, hung this maxim, borrowed from the wisdom of Joseph Prudhomme: "Without order nothing happens."

The said maxim served as an epigraph for the posters of the representations, given "by order," since without order nothing happens.

There were many inscriptions around the house. Tenants and visitors all had the epigraphic spirit. Each piece therefore had a specific, justifiable name. On the door of the premises, it read: "Talk to Ponson," the playwright Pierre Alexis Ponson du Terrail. As a result, people entering ended up saying: "I'm going to Ponson's," instead of "I'm going to the place."

The servants of the house were two women: Tronquette, a sort of white negress, long in the service of Titine, a person of light morals who spent her heyday at the cafe called the Rat Mort (Dead Rat), later working for Amédée Rolland, and a few other men of letters. Tronquette was responsible for making the beds for these gentlemen, but her main occupation was never to wash her hands or face. Auguste de Chatillon asked her one day if she was washing anything else; Tronquette replied: "Come and see!" Leonidas's wife would have said, "Come and get it."

The other woman was the cook, Aimée—similar to all cooks imaginable.

Aimée and Tronquette slept together in a small veranda at the entrance to the garden, on the door of which was written: "Speak to Tronquette."

Albert Glatigny was surprised one day in this veranda, seeing the two silly geese violently pulsating in the pleasures of lesbianism. Tronquette's virtue was manifested at this moment in the form of a broomstick, which she brandished over the head, the real "head," of this immoral but convicted poet.

Each thing, each animal in the garden had a particular name, intended to mislead strangers about its nature and origin:

The well was called—*The Source of the Nile*;

A cesspool—*The Hippocrene*;

A sandy area, reserved for making weapons—*The Field of Mars*;

The dog cage—*The Menagerie*;

Follette, poodle bitch—*Atlas's Lioness*;

Pip, rat dog—*Bengal Tiger*;

A stuffed cat, chained to the top of the well—*Monkey from Peru, brought back by Captain Camil*;

The hen cage bore this inscription— *Cock of Gruyere, given by the French consul to Batignolles*;

A black magpie, with cropped wings, which hopped here and there, had been baptized *Black Pearl*, in honor of Victorien Sardou's play;

The trees bore similar tags:

An apricot tree—Sausage-Maker with garlic, given by Mr. Champfleury;

A fir tree— Road through the Alps, given by M. de Lamartine;

A plum tree— Common Cubeb (Climbing Plant), given by Miss Suzanne Lagier.

On the walls stretched a fresco painted by Lemercier de Neuville, depicting a performance hall where masses of spectators, exceedingly true to life, lounged in the boxes. The stage, at the back of the room, was no less than sixteen feet deep, and was engineered in such a way as to represent extravaganzas as complicated as *The Deer in the Woods*. The staff included Amédée Rolland (Landlord and owner); Lemercier de Neuville (Privileged Director); Jean Duboys (General Manager); and Camille Weinschenck (Lamp operator, machinist, in a word all of the lowly functions). The material designed for the theatrical productions included eight dolls, sculpted by Demarsy, actor at the Porte-Saint-Martin theatre; twelve costumes, executed by the mistresses of the members of the administration; thirty-six sets, painted by Edmond Witersheim and Lemercier de Neuville, but retouched by Darjou, who painted the facade of the theatre; two decors, the Louis XV salon and the kitchen, which were used in *Dollar Sign*, were the work of

Victor Margaine, the happy mortal to whom Madame Alphonsine of the Variétés theatre once said: "Be my Caius, I will be your Caia!"

Let us move on to the list of the works represented at this theatre during the summer of 1862 and the winter of 1863, at the end of which, because of the relocation of Amédée Rolland, the Erotikon Theatron closed its doors:

1. *Erotikon Theatron*, prologue in verse, by Jean Duboys;

2. *Dollar Sign*, vaudeville in three acts, by the same author;

3. *The Last Day of a Condemned Man*, drama in three acts, by Tisserant;

4. *A Caprice*, vaudeville in one act, by Lemercier de Neuville;

5. *The Games of Love and the Marketplace*, comedy of manners, by the same author;

6. *The Grisette and the Student*, comedy in one act, by Henry Monnier;

7. *Scapin Pimp*, drama in two acts, in verse, by Albert Glatigny.

A newspaper of the time, the *Boulevard*, gave the account of the first performance, in its issue of June 1, 1862: "Another new theatre! an intimate *Erotikon Theatron* theatre, which is to say, an *Amorous Puppet Theatre*. Rest assured, everything is going as smoothly as possible; thrashings are always protective of morality, and if a mother cannot take her daughter there, the pleasurable theatre performance attracts talented painters and literary men.

"The facade of the theatre, painted by Darjou, deserves a special description—but Prologus will fill my task—Prologus, that is to say a buffoon character, for whom Jean Duboys created charming verses, which we cannot quote entirely, for lack of space, but here is a sample:

Gentlemen, greetings; greetings, ladies;

The graceful, and the passionate,

The brilliant and the beautiful,

The staff of this spectacle,

Tonight, are about to make their debut

Before your double majesties.

It will not lack zeal—

But, as well as the young lady

Called Anna Bellangé,
This rather crazy staff
Has not appeared in any theatre
And desires to be encouraged.

So, kindly hide your drilled keys,
No exaggerated clamor,
In which you faithfully imitate
A thousand sounds of nature,
From storms and thunder
To dogs and their barks.

We rely on your wisdom
So that no one transgresses
This slight warning,
And even in our department,
We've omitted the police,
For fear of offending you.

Our new theatre has incurred enormous costs—
Be assured that everything is newly painted—
Harlequin hovering lets you admire his figure,
And Jourdain his shiny, waxed shoes.

Pierrot dangling makes a face,
And with his googly eye,
He contemplates a double bass,
Next to the pot he looted.

See them wrap around their heads
Vines mixed with laurel,
Sacred branches that poets

Especially like to embrace.

In addition, our privilege
Admits all genres: ballets—
Women's plays, and their retinue
Of short petticoats and calves—
And cannon drama, if I wanted!

"As you can see, these puppets are quite literary; Darjou also painted the facade of the theatre with no less artistry than Jean Duboys described it. We pay him our sincere compliments."

This first performance was followed by a grand supper, at which Champfleury raised this audacious toast: "To the death of the Théâtre-Français! To the prosperity of the Puppets!"

Today, nothing remains of this theatre but a memory of gaiety and madness.

Conservatives have settled in the house in the rue de la Santé—the frescoes are covered with whitewash—and the authors of the jolly antics that you are about to read, engage in the composition of serious works, in order to deserve the penalty of the Académie-Française in perpetuity.

Dollar Sign
(1862)
Vaudeville in Three Acts
by
Amédée Rolland and Jean Duboys

According to the preface to the published play, the comedy was performed on May 27, 1862 for the inauguration of the Erotic Theatre. The only author named was Jean Duboys, but the play was a collaborative effort with Amédée Rolland. An excess of modesty prevented Rolland, the author of the Doctor's Vacation, *from having his name proclaimed.*

The play was a great success despite the length of the intermissions. To induce the spectators to be patient, Charles Monselet, played, between the first and the second act, scenes from the Gentleman whose Seat has been taken. *This interlude was greeted by a thunderous wave of applause.*

In the third act, the public was deeply impressed by the appearance of a genuine five-hundred-franc bank note. The puppet in charge of the role of Marquis, playing with this note, having imprudently approached a lighted candle, Amédée Rolland, at the risk of disturbing the spectacle and jeopardizing the success of the work, sprung up, and cried out, like the trumpet of Judgment: "In the name of God! take care not to burn it!"

Taking advantage of the emotion caused by this spectacular incident, Monselet (again!) rushed to the stage, and tried to strip the note from the puppet. A violent murmur of reprobation rose from the four corners of the room, and made the author of Morpion Etruscan *understand that he would find judges among the spectators, since he had neglected to look there for friends.*

During the performance, Poulet-Malassis did not cease to jeopardize himself, ostensibly washing the dishes from Mademoiselle Tronquette's (unwashed) hands. No doubt that by the exercise of prolonged linguistics in the kitchen scene, the giblets of this new Mauritian cuisine would have become comparable to those of the northern climates—but the refreshments did not circulate. This scene exemplified the literary focus of the Erotic Theatre for, in preparing a plate of excrement for his wife, the Marquis seasons the dish with flavors that evoke a critique of poets and playwrights, including Ariosto (1474–1533), Aretino (1492–1556), Molière (1622–1673), Nicolas La Grange (1707–1775), Philippe-Laurent Pons de Verdun (1759–1844), Clairville [Louis-François-Marie Nicolaïe] (1811–1879), Armand de Pontmartin (1811–1890), Adolphe Dennery (1811–1899), François Ponsard (1814–1867), Jules Moineaux (1815–1895), Jean-Baptiste Cochinat (1819–1886), Théodore de Banville (1823–1891), Alfred Delvau (1825–1867), Charles Monselet (1825–1888), Hector-Jonathan Crémieux (1828–1893), Pierre Alexis Ponson du Terrail (1829–1871), and Victorien Sardou (1831–1908).

Dollar Sign *was given five performances.*

Characters

The Marquis de Coquencu
The Marchioness de Coquencu
Germain, servant to the Marquis, fucker of the Marchioness
A Soldier in the Italian army
A Peddler of bad books

Act One

(*The action takes place in a French salon.*)

Marquis. Thus, the noble name of Coquencu would die out! In vain I work as a conscientious winegrower in the conjugal vineyard—in vain I weed and hoe—for ten years Madame de Coquencu has not shown the slightest traces of fertility! The blood of Venus, to use the poetic expression of Sire de Banville, flows in abundance from its natural wound.

(*Sings, to the tune of "I live on the fourth floor."*)
My wife, although nervous,
Never has the vapors;
Her health, still vigorous,
Has not, per her pale color,
Suffered more than the sniffles;
And really, I venture
In a place that I know—
She may say to me: Take—*care*!
Me, I only take her—in the ass!

(*Spoken.*) My wife's nervous attacks are usually simulated and are not followed by any kind of vomiting. This utter absence of symptoms demonstrates, in a deplorably precise way, that I will not yet have an heir this year— It will not be said however that a Coquencu will not have made every effort to perpetuate his race, and today, I will have one last try! Hola! Anybody! (*He goes to ring at the back.*) Germain—

Germain. (*Entering.*) Sir, the Marquis rang?

Marquis. Ask Madame de Coquencu to come and join me here. (*Germain bows and exits.*) This supreme interview will decide the fate of my illustrious race. O, Népomucène Coquencu! Glorious knight of the crusades, inspire your humble descendant! Give him courage! Give him courage!! Give him courage!!!

Marchioness. (*Entering.*) You wanted to see me, Monsieur le Marquis?

Marquis. (*Tenderly.*) Yes, pretty lady. We have to chat about things—serious things—

Marchioness. (*Simpering.*) Oh, Marquis! Serious things!

Marquis. (*More and more tender.*) About things exceedingly—serious—

Marchioness. (*Curious.*) I'm listening.

Marquis. (*While questioning his pants.*) Madam—(*Aside.*) I don't know how to tell her that, I—

Marchioness. (*Who wants to know.*) Come on, sir, come on! You're unbearable with your retentions—of language.

Marquis. (*That the response of his pants was unsatisfactory.*) Madam—Hem! Hem! It's very embarrassing, word of honor! Madam—

Marchioness. Sir?

Marquis. (*Finding a solution.*) Do you still have those excellent lozenges that you made me take in the early days of our marriage?

Marchioness. (*With modesty.*) What! Sir. Do you desire—

Marquis. (*Whose cock has just stirred nicely.*) Exactly. I desire! O, Ernestine, have you already forgotten our tenderness?

Marchioness. (*Inflamed by this movement which catches her by surprise.*) My Jules! Here is my pill box. (*She gives him her pill box.*)

Marquis. (*Seizing it voraciously.*) Thank you, queen of my loves! (*Aside.*) A little Spanish fly never hurts. (*Sings, to the tune of "Masaniello."*)

Spanish fly belongs to Kythera

In use, like in Paris;

Its effect is very beneficial,

Especially for us husbands,

This candy turns me into Alcide!

I was so weak beforehand—

Ahead of the Spanish fly!

Yes, the Spanish fly ahead!

(*He hurriedly swallows a pill.*)

Marchioness. (*Who follows his every move with interest.*) Take two, my angel—

Marquis. (*Eagerly taking a second pill.*) Yes, my idol!

Marchioness. (*Aside.*) And to think that he absolutely needs these kinds of things! Germain is doing quite well, himself—

Marquis. (*Whose prick is silent again.*) If you were to go get the quills—my dove?

Marchioness. (*Resigned.*) Yes, my pigeon, if you desire it. (*False exit.*)

Marquis. (*Sings, to the tune of "Bastien's Boots."*)
But I would also like, Marchioness,
This preparation of the peacock,
When the feather, under my shirt,
Caresses my hanging "purse."
Alas! do I have to say it?
My happiness depends on this peacock—

Marchioness. Be satisfied, my friend. (*She puts a peacock feather between his buttocks.*)

Marquis. (*Walking around, doing a cartwheel, but without having an erection.*)
Oh! the pretty peacock! The pretty peacock,
Pan, pan,
Who's making pan, pan,
Pan, pan,
On my hanging purse!
If on the peacock
Depends
My pleasure, it's that a peacock,
This dapper animal,
To Venus made pan, pan!

Marchioness. (*Running her hand over his back, to make him horny.*) Oh! the beautiful peacock! How sweet is this beautiful peacock!—What a beautiful cocktail, this beautiful peacock!—

Marquis. (*Sensing that he's becoming aroused.*) Again!—Again!—

Marchioness. (*Skillfully making a spider's web.*) Oh! God! the beautiful peacock! The beautiful peacock!—The beautiful peacock!—

Marquis. (*Who gradually stiffens.*) It's going up!

Marchioness. (*Hastening her manipulations.*) Oh! The beautiful peacock!—The beautiful peacock!—

Marquis. (*Who managed to get hard.*) Enough!—enough!—enough!—Ah! what pleasure!—

Marchioness. (*Caressing his member carefully, for fear of breaking it.*) Oh! the beautiful peacock!—What do we have here, little rascal?

Marquis. (*Rowing.*) O, Ernestine! I love you! I—I—I—love—you. (*He sings, while covering the Marchioness with fiery kisses, from the throat to the navel. Tune: "One day at the gate."*)

Let my mouth go astray—

Marchioness. (*Lowering his head in the direction she wants it to go. Singing.*) Lower, lower—

Marquis. (*Split between the desire for oral sex and that of jerking her off.*)

Let my middle finger touch you—

Marchioness. (*Still lowering his head.*) Lower, lower—

Marquis. (*Same action.*) Do you feel my sweet lips?

Marchioness. (*Same action.*) Lower, lower—

Marquis. (*Swooning.*) I'm burning, I have a fever—

Marchioness. (*Same action.*) So, go lower—

(*Speaking.*) Oh! Jules—Jules—be careful!

Marquis. (*His head buried in the pleasant lawn of the Marchioness, and working his tongue energetically. Speaking*) What?

Marchioness. (*Modestly.*) You're going to eat my fruit—

Marquis. (*Withdrawing his head and tongue.*) Your fruit? But then—it could be true—O, Ernestine! No false joy! Could it be true that I am going to be a father?

Marchioness. (*Leading his hand as she led his head.*) Touch, Marquis—

Marquis. (*Feeling.*) This is the moment to come up with a phrase—Yes! Yes! I feel it palpitating in your sacred flanks, the Coquencu of the future! Yes! Yes! Yes! It throbs.

Marchioness. (*Brusquely.*) We'll send him to the Polytechnic Institute! You want to?

Marquis. (*Delighted.*) He will join the army, which is a way of fucking women—

Marchioness. (*Changing her mind.*) Or he will go into law, like his great-uncle.

Marquis. (*With a noble disdain.*) Fie! Marchioness! Fie! The last Coquencu will not be a judge.

Marchioness. (*Getting excited.*) Yes! Monsieur le Marquis, I insist!

Marquis. (*With dignity.*) Huh! What's there to say?

Marchioness. (*Becoming exasperated.*) You're violating me!

Marquis. (*Surprised.*) Me?

Marchioness. (*Who does all she can to cry.*) You're a tyrant!

Marquis. (*More and more surprised, and buttoning himself up so as not to show his penis, really ashamed at the moment.*) But, Madam de Coquencu—

Marchioness. (*The same.*) And we don't treat an unhappy pregnant woman like that—

Marquis. (*Trying to calm her.*) Listen to me—

Marchioness. (*The same.*) No—no—no! I want to become angry!

Marquis. (*Begging.*) Ernestine!

Marchioness. (*The same action.*) It will spoil my fruit—so much the better—

Marquis. (*More and more pleading.*) Please!

Marchioness. (*At the height of exasperation.*) And if you're not happy, this is for you! (*She beats him like a beast in a barn.*)

Marquis. (*Fleeing.*) Ouch!—ouch!—ouch!—

Marchioness. (*Swooning.*) Ah! God! The wicked man!—the wicked man!—

Marquis. (*Returning to her to try to console her.*) What! it's me who—and it's she who—

Marchioness. (*Sobbing.*) I'll die! Some air—air—Ah!—(*Simulated nervous attack.*)

Marquis. (*In great agitation.*) Oh! my God! What to do? Toinon! Germain! She's going to spoil her fruit—she will spoil it—she mustn't spoil it—I've had too much trouble having it! We must save it—we must save the last of Coquencu—Toinon! Germain! See if those scoundrels will come! Toinon! Germain! Salts! vinegar! pepper! oil! (*He exits, running and calling, as if he's lost his head, his hands raised to the sky. Enter Germain.*)

Germain. (*Looking at the Marchioness, who has passed out, and smiling. Tune from "Saltarello."*)

(*Sings.*) Yes, I know that; it's madam

Who takes on her little roguish attitude;

She needs, the dear wife,

My way, in a way;

She's only at her ease

When her husband is away—

Then, here's one who wants to be fucked—

It's true that women are made for that.

(*He approaches her, kneels, lifts her dress and her petticoats, spreads her thighs, and begins to fuck her. While fucking the Marchioness, he continues to sing.*)

Yes, I know that— it's madam—

Who takes on— her little—roguish attitude—

She needs—the dear wife—

My way—in a way.

Marchioness. (*While quivering under Germain.*)

(*Sings.*) You know—me—I am your—lady—

I take on—my little—roguish attitude—

And you—Germain—I claim—

One way—your—way—

End of Act One.

Act Two

(*The scene is a landscape from the Realistic School of painting. An Italian soldier on sentry duty and a peddler are squatting at the corners of the stage.*)

Soldier. (*Defecating easily.*) One! Deuce! It's a honey!

Peddler. (*Who is constipated.*) Ouch! As long as things last, I'll spend all my savings on laxatives—

Soldier. (*Cheerfully pushing out one last turd.*) Hey! say, old man! you seem to me to be in a bad mood?

Peddler. (*Who pushes out his first log with difficulty.*) I believe it! Everything's going from bad to worse for us peddlers.—I wasn't already selling so many books—now they are ruining us with their stamp! They can only imagine, word of honor! Ouch!—it's so hard!

Soldier. (*He gets up and pulls up his trousers.*) What a pleasure, eh! to put his shit on the grass?

Peddler. (*Getting up too, but without finishing his* shit.) It is obvious that you're carefree, you—

Soldier. And what concern should I have, in the name of God! Am I not covered with glory, neither more nor less than the rest of the French army? (*Sings, to the tune of "The Montmartre Recruit."*)

We took Sebastopol,

Delivered Italy;

We purged the ground

Call Syria;

We came back from China;

In Mexico we Mexi-could!

We're gay dogs,

And everywhere we shit

Without being asked!

Peddler. (*Melancholy because of his constipation.*) Literature is in the doldrums—

Soldier. (*Who, while getting dressed, contemplates his shit, with satisfaction.*) The Austrians have to pay to rub themselves in the countryside!

Peddler. (*Mumbling.*) Nothing but *Madame Charbonneau's Thursdays* in my bag!

Soldier. (*Radiant.*) A hearty stool, I dare say! Marshal Bigturd would have been happy!

Peddler. (*More and more enraged by his constipation. Ironically.*) A fantastic warm-up!

Soldier. (*Same action.*) Everything is going the best in the world!

Peddler. (*More and more enraged by his constipation.*) Things are at their worst!

Soldier. (*After a last look of satisfaction cast upon his turd.*) Here it is! The best, an antique! (*He exits.*)

Peddler. Well! I'll follow you—I might be luckier behind the next bush. (*He picks up his bundle and walks away with the soldier. Enter the Marquis and Marchioness from up right.*)

Marchioness. O, Jules! What a delicious spot! Let's stop here—you want to?

Marquis. (*Submissive, like a man happy that he's soon to be a father.*) You know, Ernestine, that I'm a slave to your desires.

Marchioness. (*Approaching the place where the soldier took a shit.*) What a charming smell one breathes in this grove! Undoubtedly that of the flowers in these meadows—

Marquis. (*Covering his nose in disgust.*) I think it stinks horribly, myself!

Marchioness. (*In a reproachful tone.*) O, Jules! You're so mundane!

Marquis. (*Who persists in his disgust.*) I am not mundane; I think it smells bad: that's all—

Marchioness. (*Sniffing, as if in a bed of roses.*) Myself, I think it smells good! And I want you to think it smells good!

Marquis. (*Protesting.*) However, dear friend—

Marchioness. (*Upset.*) Oh! My nerves! My nerves!

Marquis. (*Alarmed.*) Good Lord! and my child whom the slightest displeasure could kill!

(*Sings, to the tune of "Admiral Cornarini."*)

Let's not bother the fruit

That is produced

In her tiny room!

It's crawling, crawling, crawling, crawling, crawling again—

This child,

Who, triumphant,

Must come out of her noble flank,

With me already con, con, con, con, contributing—

Yes, of course, a Coquencu

Will come out of her cunt.

(*Deciding, in spite of himself, to share the opinion of the Marchioness. Speaking*) Yes, dear friend, you're right: this smell is delicious—

Marchioness. (*Radiantly.*) Finally!

Marquis. (*With conviction and gagging.*) And yet it stinks. (*He walks in the soldier's shit.*) There! Like I was saying!

Marchioness. (*Sweetly.*) What, my friend?

Marquis. (*Showing her the soldier's turds.*) Dollar sign!

Marchioness. (*With reproach.*) Oh! Fie! Marquis—

Marquis. (*Surprised.*) What?

Marchioness. (*Scandalized.*) Your expressions are vulgar!

Marquis. Damn! at least the words don't stink, and you thought earlier that the thing itself smelled good.

Marchioness. (*With bitterness.*) Reproaches now! Ah! how unhappy I am!

Marquis. Please, calm yourself.

Marchioness, (*Uneasy, and crying.*) Oh! Oh! Oh!

Marquis. (*Trying to appease her.*) There! There! There!—my little hen—

Marchioness. (*Swooning.*) My bottle! I forgot my bottle!

Marquis. (*Embarrassed.*) She feels bad. What to do?

Marchioness. (*Shuddering, annoyed.*) Please, a perfume! It doesn't matter which—a perfume!

Marquis. (*Looking at his feet, where lies the "egg" laid by the soldier.*) What an idea! (*He indicates, with an eloquent gesture, his reluctance to grasp the above-mentioned perfume.*)

Marchioness. (*Still swooning.*) Oh! I'm suffering—I'm suffering!

Marquis. (*Full of anxiety.*) And no paper!

Peddler. (*Entering.*) It wasn't any more successful! *Madame Charbonneau's Thursdays* bring me bad luck.

Marquis. (*Lighting up.*) Hey! Good man—are you selling books?

Peddler. Yes, sir, at your service. Which one would you like?

Marquis. (*Briskly.*) Oh! It doesn't matter which, for what I'm going to do with it.

Peddler. (*Unpacking his merchandise.*) I have just what you need—

Marquis. Give me, give me! (*The peddler gives him a book, in exchange for which the Marquis gives him a purse.*) Here!

Peddler. (*Walking away.*) Luck seems to be turning—Let's go into this thicket and try again to give birth from behind.

Marquis. (*With a marked repulsion.*) This smell would wake up the dead! (*Nonetheless, he bends down towards the soldier's turd, grasps it carefully, wraps it delicately, and presents it to the nose of the marchioness.*)

Marchioness. (*Shuddering pleasantly.*) Ah! ah! ah! the delicious smell—

Marquis. (*Amazed at this result.*) Strange perversion of smell in pregnant women! Oh! nature! who can know all your oddities—Amazing! amazing! amazing!

Marchioness. (*Completely coming back to her senses.*) I feel better. So, you have found my bottle!

Marquis. (*Embarrassed.*) Yes—yes—

Marchioness. Don't misplace it, please—I'm still so weak—I have to smell it all the time—

Marquis. (*Aside.*) What! I have to carry it! (*Aloud.*) Be careful, dear friend—you must not abuse strong—odors—

Marchioness. You're still going to contradict me?

Marquis. No—no!

Marchioness. Then—to the hotel!

Marquis. No! To the nearest house I'll hasten to get rid of this—this—

Marchioness. Quickly—quickly!

Marquis. Oh! Pregnant women! If I had known, I would have done like Saturn: I would have eaten my child. (*Sings, to the tune of "Pleasant boys and girls."*)

This perfume

That does not smell of amber

I will get rid of

In the first house

I'll come across!

Marchioness. (*Singing.*) But it smells very nice.

Marquis. I don't think so!

Marchioness. Yes.

Marquis. No.

Marchioness. Yes.

Marquis. No.

End of Act Two.

Act Three

Marquis. (*Alone.*) For an hour, in despair, I have kept this overly odorous perfume in my pocket—My valets, in the car, turn their heads and sniff knowingly—A swarm of flies of all colors swirls around me, and a dung beetle fell down into the pocket of my jacket—This situation is unbearable! (*Sings, to the tune of "Women, do you want to try."*)

A big pig that was eating

In the courtyard of this cottage,

Came out, head first,

From the quagmire that covered it

And smelling the fatal odor,

He comes running like the wind—

On my honor, the pig wanted

To eat the slop from my clothes.

(*Speaking.*) But, luckily, I was able to escape the Marchioness's active surveillance for a minute. I feigned an urgent need, and I am going, quite at my ease, to get rid of this unpleasant package. Let's see—or could I hide it? (*He searches carefully for a hiding place.*)

Marchioness. Well! my friend, this is how you leave me alone!

Marquis. Ouch! The Marchioness! (*He tries to conceal his package.*)

Marchioness. (*Noticing his awkwardness.*) What are you hiding, Jules?

Marquis. (*More and more disconcerted.*) Nothing, Ernestine—Nothing at all—

Marchioness. (*Sulky.*) Ah! you no longer love me, since you're keeping secrets from me—

Marquis. (*Sincerely.*) I swear to you—

Marchioness. (*Melancholy.*) Poor being, who throbs in my entrails, you will have only an unnatural father!

Marquis. (*Completely perplexed.*) Where will I hide it? My God! where will I hide it?

Marchioness. (*Who thinks she can guess.*) The mystery in which you surround yourself gives me a singular suspicion—

Marquis. (*Quickly.*) I assure you it's nothing—

Marchioness. Ah! I guess—I can feel it—it's about a rival!

Marquis. (*With disgust.*) Ugh! A rival of Madame Domange, perhaps, but of you! Oh!

Marchioness. (*Urgently.*) Jules, show me the contents of that paper!

Marquis. (*Pleading.*) Please—

Marchioness. (*In a tone that admits of no reply.*) I want to see it—

Marquis. (*In a bad mood.*) Hey! what the devil, madam?

Marchioness. (*Violently.*) I want to see it—I want to see it! (*Gently.*) My God! It's a woman's whim, my friend. Yield! What do you care if you're not guilty? (*Bursting.*) Monsieur le Marquis, I want to see the contents of that paper!

Marquis. (*Pushed to the limit.*) So, be satisfied, Marchioness. (*Unfolding business, full of precautions first, smells afterwards.*)

Marchioness. (*At the height of astonishment.*) What do I see?

Marquis. Ugh! (*He sneezes.*)

Marchioness. (*Same action.*) How can you have such things in your pocket?

Marquis. What! It was you, yourself, who—

Marchioness. (*Same action.*) Me?—Me?—Me?—

Marquis. (*In a bad mood.*) Undoubtedly, madam.

Marchioness. (*Hurt.*) Marquis! You're impertinent!

Marquis. (*Hurt also.*) Marquise! you are one—one—one—inconsistent woman! Since this morning you have had strange whims, which I am constantly forced to satisfy, and when I satisfy them, you still reproach me—

Marchioness. (*Crying and becoming tense.*) Oh! my God! how unhappy I am!

Marquis. (*Ironically.*) Ah! you know—no attacks of nerves! I know that one now—

Marchioness. (*Stunned*) "I know"? What do you know?

Marquis. (*Same action.*) You don't put it over on me anymore, I warn you— (*Sings, to the tune of "Bertha's Piano."*)

You don't put it over on me anymore,

You don't put it over on me anymore,

So, your efforts will be in vain!

You have put it over on me too long, madame;

For you I have only a remnant of passion--

You don't put it over on me anymore,

You don't put it over on me anymore!

Marchioness. (*At the height of indignation.*) We don't put it over on him any more—have we already put it over on him? So, the man whom I honored with my favors would have unnatural tastes? We don't put it over on him anymore! Ah! Dare to speak this slang in front of me! Dare to disrespect me at this point—to treat me like the last of the last! I will avenge myself! Yes!

Marquis. (*Still ironically.*) Pass out, if you want—I don't care—

Marchioness. (*On the verge of bursting, suddenly changing her mind.*) What an idea! (*Softly.*) Oh! marquis of my heart, little marquis, nice marquis, my only friend, listen to your little wife who loves you, who will caress you, pamper you, be nice to you, and love you until the end of your days!

Marquis. (*Sensitive to her cajoling.*) At the right time—

Marchioness. (*Tenderly.*) Great big Jules would not like to cause great big grief for his Nestine, would he?

Marquis. (*Tenderly as well.*) No! No! No!

Marchioness. (*Cuddling him as she would Germain.*) Good bunny, good little darling, kiss mama!

Marquis. (*Half-vanquished.*) Of course—

Marchioness. (*Same action.*) Little two-penny puppy to his beloved granny—

Marquis. (*Three-quarter-vanquished.*) I'm not saying no—

Marchioness. (*Same action.*) And now granny has a big, big desire, as big as she is fat--

Marquis. (*Quite vanquished.*) Tell me what you want, Marchioness.

Marchioness. (*Same action.*) Promise me, my dear wolf, that you will submit to it? I will tell you later—You know that a desire is very serious for a pregnant woman—

Marquis. (*Who is almost as erect as Germain.*) Go on, seductress! Delilah!

Marchioness. (*Same action.*) What did you say, my chick?

Marquis. I said: Delilah!

Marchioness. (*Same action.*) I'll be very nice—you'll see—

Marquis. (*Who is quite as hard as Germain.*) Well, so be it! I promise—

Marchioness. Say: I swear on my word as a gentleman!

Marquis. My word as a gentleman!

Marchioness. By the noble name of Coquencu!

Marquis. By the illustrious name of Coquencu!

Marchioness. To submit to the wishes of my little wife—

Marquis. (*Who thinks it's a little trip to Kythera.*) I swear. And this desire—

Marchioness. (*Quietly.*) Oh, my God! It is very simple. (*Showing him the soldier's turd.*) Cook it.

Marquis. (*Who thinks he's misheard.*) Huh?

Marchioness. (*Repeating, with the same serenity.*) Cook it.

Marquis. (*With noble indignation.*) Never!

Marchioness. (*With contemptuous irony.*) So, you're breaking your oath! O, Coquencus of the past! I appeal to you for the disgrace of Coquencu present!

Marquis. (*Troubled.*) It's true, I swore—

Marchioness. (*Wanting to take advantage of his concern.*) Let's go to the kitchen—

Marquis. (*Same action.*) But still—I would like to know the reason—

Marchioness. The reason?

Marquis. Yes.

Marchioness. (*With a simplicity worthy of ancient times.*) The reason? I want to eat it.

Marquis. (*Unable to believe his ears.*) You—

Marchioness. Me—I desire it—

Marquis. (*Same action.*) But it's outrageous!

Marchioness. (*In a tone that does not admit of a reply.*) A pregnant woman's desire is sacred! Your son would have it at the tip of his nose—(*She exits majestically, after indicating the soldier's turd for the last time.*)

Marquis. (*Resigned.*) That argument convinces me—but—there's no kitchen here—

(*Sings, to a medley of famous tunes.*)
Ah! I see a library,
As a kitchen it can serve me—
Near Louvet, I see Seneca placed there,
And Blum and Flan next to Sappho—

But for my choice, everything really puzzles me—
Let's take bay leaves first:
This *Aminta* will serve as my cup,
This Aretino is worth a whole pepper tree.

In terms of salt, I see here Molière;
I see Clairville—oh! But it's coarse salt!
Grangé, Thiboust, in the same salt cellar,
With Crémieux, are present at the call—

This Monselet will serve as nutmeg,
If you like it, I'll use it everywhere;
So that my dish does not remain bland,
I'm, once more, adding this clove: Babou!

Let's tie it all together with a string:
At Dennery's I find it, in faith;
But a happy author, I believe, is calling me,
And flutters abundantly around me.

It's you, Sardou! it is you, covered with glory,
Pearl, jewel—of brilliant success,
Well! Sardou, despite your *Black Pearl*,
I'll take you for a burnt onion—

What then? Garlic, which is wrongly rejected,
Is a real perfume, when, skillfully,
It can be combined with red sauce:
The best garlic comes to us from Molinchart!

Let's add Banville, whose cream
Did not sour, despite the bad weather;
And to tie together this supreme sauce,
Let's break this egg: Molineaux will be in it.

A little Alfred Delvau, very little, could do no harm:
His *Loves* are unhealthy, but by cooking them—
The *Dramas from Paris*, by Ponson du Terrail,
Will have a very good effect on this casserole;
Pontmartin! his *Thursdays*—of course! Here's the garlic—
I've already used it, but what consoles me,
It is that a little more garlic will only be a detail.

Oh! Oh! here are the epigrams
From the so-called Pons de Verdun!
Epigrams of lamb go well with *Dramas
From Paris*—that's perfect!—Let's move on! Another,
To spice up these epigrams:
Alas! what do I see! the *Old Cunt!*—
This title seems weird to me,
Even more than the *Erotikon*:
Let's read it again—the *Old Country*
Ah! *try*! I understand! and my mind goes astray;
In any sauce you need water:
The *Old Cunt* and Ponroy are quite rare—
Ponsard!—the case is improper!
Everything is declining,

Nothing is missing from this routine,
Nominative or genitive:
Pons, Ponson, Pontmartin, Ponroy, Ponsard, Ponsif!

Now a little vinegar:
Lacenaire, by Cochinat;
Ah! no, that's not barley,
The black prose of that negro!

A small bunch of parsley:
The *Black Talons*, which Jaime wrote:
I believe that's enough for me;
Yet the onion's still missing.

Ah! let's peel the *Grace of God*—
It makes me cry—lord knows!
Yet instead of it, a little bit, I'd choose,
Between us, a banknote—

Hell! take *Pulkriska,*
And avoid the outcome at *Paillasse*:
The work of two pedigree authors
Isn't designed for poo.

Jean Coutandier? Isn't that shifty!
The Usurer?—I don't dare!
Gaetana I don't touch:
What would Ribe and Mosé think!

Here is Sarcelle de Gouttière,
Gibier, very lean game, in truth,
But we have a matter

Sufficiently fat on the side—

What more could I add?
Ah! that old broom—Dennery!
Or G. Claudin who's been decorated !!!!
Then *The Husband's Revenge*.

Grab Gandon, that old saber
Which Bourdillat brandishes in vain;
Add this "Cunt-de-Labre"—
Let's canonize that swindler;
It's finished—No, that dandy—Jouvin!

Yes, yes, really this library,
As a kitchen, here, can serve me:
I won't find rhyme on horseback here,
But enough to satisfy my desire—
(*While singing, the marquis has made the dish of shit intended for his wife; when it is ready, he brings it in, shouting.*) Here it is, Marchioness!

Marchioness. (*Returning immediately.*) This dish looks really good; Marquis, I congratulate you.

Marquis. (*Who would like to earn more praise.*) Uh! uh!

Marchioness. You seem to doubt it—

Marquis. (*Defending himself.*) Me? no certainly—

Marchioness. Then, will you keep me company?

Marquis. (*Politely.*) I fear you won't have enough left—

Marchioness. (*Insisting.*) Please, Marquis, no inflated discretion! Since I'm inviting you to share this treat with me, it will be nice—

Marquis. (*Still resisting.*) I swear I'm not hungry!

Marchioness. (*As if suddenly suspicious.*) Ah! I'm guessing everything—you want to get rid of me! I have been weighing you down for a long time—this dish is poisoned!

Marquis. (*Sings, to the tune of "He was a little man."*)

I know it poisons,

But it's not, no, no,

Poison;

At least the person

Who made this thing,

Without worry,

Made it,

And deposited it

Where my nose found it,

Wasn't poi—

Wasn't poi—

Poisoned too!

Marchioness. (*Who sticks to her idea.*) Then, to prove your innocence—taste it!

Marquis. (*Declining.*) But—

Marchioness. Taste it, taste it, I tell you—taste it, then, marquis—(*She thrusts his head in the dish.*)

Marquis. (*His mouth full.*) But—Madam de Coquencu—

Marchioness. (*Walking away, uttering peacock cries.*) Fie! you ugly man! Stay away from me—you stink! I'll complain to my mother—I don't want to be united with a monster who eats such abominations! Go away! Go away! Go immediately!

Marquis. (*His mouth dredged with flour.*) Madam?

Marchioness. (*With anger, disgust and contempt.*) Don't follow me! I don't want to see you anymore! (*She goes out.*)

Marquis. (*Getting rid of the shit as best he can.*) What! She doesn't want to see me anymore! I'm going crazy— (*He gestures, he cries. He sings, to the tune of the "Baker."*)

Ah! I'm going crazy!

I don't know how far

My madness can go!

Cabbages, leeks, turnips, celery—(*Tremolo in the orchestra. Recitative spoken.*)

Around me I see moist Spanish flies—Pontmartin casseroles—Hi! hi! hi! from Ponson—Oh! Ernestine, Ernestine! Ah! Thank you, my God! There she is! (*He grabs the turd, holds it up and cries out.*) Mine! Montjoye and Coquencu! (*He disappears singing.*)

Ah! I'm going crazy!
I don't know how far
My madness can go!
Wow! wow! I'm going crazy, I'm going crazy,
And I've come a cropper!

The End.

The Games of Love and the Marketplace (1862-1863) Comedy of Manners in One Act by Lemercier de Neuville

A satire of The Game of Love and Chance *by Pierre de Marivaux,* The Games of Love and the Marketplace *was one of the great successes of the Erotic Theatre. In the Marivaux play, a woman of the upper class, expecting to meet her fiancé (whom she had never seen), pretends to be her maid so that she can discover the true character of the man she is about to marry, unaware that her upper-class betrothed, is pretending to be his valet so that he can discover the true nature of his bride. Neuville transforms the upper-class characters of Marivaux's comedy into a Madam and a Pimp—the upper-class figures in a brothel—who pretend to be a prostitute and a john to engage in a feisty game of foreplay.*

According to the advertisement for The Games of Love and the Marketplace, *Lemercier de Neuville was in direct contravention of the association of dramatic authors by having his own works performed so often in the theatre of which he was the director, a privilege that had been granted to him. For a time, there was a question of bringing together, in a solemn assembly, the authors of the various shows in Paris, under the chairmanship of Leon Laya, to examine whether there was any need to put the Erotic Theatre under ban. A few great personages interceded, and the interdict was not pronounced.*

For the chorus of town sergeants that concluded the play, Lemercier de Neuville came up with a new trick that has since served for all the performances at the theatre. The puppets being held at the end of the arms, and the framework of the stage not being able to allow more than two people hidden behind the facade, it was of absolute necessity that there were never more than four actors on stage at the same time. On a piece of cut cardboard, Neuville painted some twenty town sergeants, who could be easily maneuvered with one hand. Each town sergeant was decorated individually.

The first performance of the Games of Love and the Marketplace *was saddened by the death of Ratapon, a fine, old, invalid cat. Although he was an atheist, he was buried the next day, in the garden, with the ceremony used by the predominant religion in France, in order to avoid the neighbors having to view the scandalous spectacle of a purely civil burial. The funeral oration for Ratapon was pronounced in these words by Mademoiselle Tronquette: "Ah well! so much the better! He won't shit on my bed anymore."*

Characters

Sylvia, a madam
Dorante, a pimp

Scene One
(The action takes place in a little room in a brothel.)
Sylvia. (*Alone. She is made up and dressed with those royal fabrics that girls use to make themselves more attractive to men. She looks at herself complacently in a mirror.*) All ready for combat! Nothing is missing that can turn on even the most "flannel" of men! I have a really dirty look for you—And this crinoline! It favors me! How good it looks on me! Here's another invention that helps us mount an attack on men—and it's a man who invented it! Oh! Dear! Dear! (*She walks in front of the mirror, continuing to look at herself, from top to bottom.*) Great idea that I had there,

all the same! It's true, it bothers you, in the end, to keep a love boutique, and not to sample your merchandise; every day to bring happiness to others and not keep a small bit for yourself; every evening, from seven o'clock to midnight, to light the candle of hymen, in favor of a heap of chicks and as many tricks, and not to spread a little of hymen's tallow on your chest; to remain here grimly, alone, idle, instead of going to the drawing room with all these ladies to talk and crack loads of jokes; to always go downstairs, and never go up. Damn! I want a guy with a big heart to go for a girl—me! I want, for one night, to rediscover the pleasures of my youth, just like my boarders! I want someone to pay me for getting paddled! I want someone to make plans for me! I want someone to smother me. I want someone to give me gloves, and fun on top of the stairs. (*The hoarse voice of someone walking outside the door: "Madam, it's yours."*) All right! Here's my turn on the tarmac. A little guy with a big heart! Someone's got to use me for the first time!

(*Sings, to the tune of "Bohemians of Paris"*)

Treading the asphalt

Of the boulevard, a lovely visit;

It is customary

To solicit day and night;

When a trick passes by,

We approach, and then, casually,

We hug him, we kiss him,

Especially if he's a handsome lad!

When we're pretty,

We can get a good price;

And this is the life,

Yes, this is the life

Of the beautiful whores of Paris. (*She exits, singing.*)

Scene Two

(*The action takes place on the street.*)

Dorante. (*Alone. He walks up and down in front of a house with a large number.*) Here's a house that I don't know. I'm surprised. Well! since my blood is beating,

I'm going to get to know it and find out what meat there is in the stall at that butcher's shop. Yes, I had an idea like that today. What? It might make me laugh a bit, to change roles, and, from pimp, to become a trick. I'm not saying that the pimp trade doesn't have its charm, especially from the point of view of the pocketbook, but there are times when it's boring, truly!—Did I get the money from you for the engagements! Oh, dear, dear! It's nothing to talk about. Yes, they're thick and wear condoms!—Nevertheless, I wouldn't mind paying *them* in turn, just to laugh and see the effect it has on me. It'll remind me, an old reprobate, of the time when I still had it, when I was so awkward with sex, when women turned me on so easily, that the first monkey who put her hand on me made me hard for two weeks. That's a long time ago, damn it!

(*Sings, to the tune of "Joseph."*)

Barely out of childhood,

Thirteen years old, a spring evening,

I followed with confidence,

A fourteen-year-old girl—

I believed, with this creature,

I would follow the lessons of Venus;

I was wrong. It was Mercury

Who pricked me with his barbs.

(*Spoken.*) A superb start! according to Mr. Ricord— Fortunately, we don't die of this more than of love. I had fourteen since that one, and of all colors, because whatever the smart ones say, venereal diseases follow one another and are not alike. And when I say the pox, I could also say the clap. I've had tarts so often! I've had 'em! So much so that I was called the King of Tarts! Well! That, however, is what gave me a taste for women, and women a taste for me. Yes! There are peasants who say that man is nourished by hope—Hope! Eh! No! It's a woman!

(*Sings, to the tune of "Queen Bacchanale."*)

I am the king of pimps!

I recognize the sucker!

At billiards, you have to see me,

I amaze real amateurs!

From Saint-Laz I know
All the brotherhood;
They allow me to earn my living
Without having to go to great expense.
Yes, it's a convenient profession
Which is also becoming fashionable:
A professional pimp,
Yes, it's a heavenly trade,
A professional pimp,
Long live the professional pimp!

(*Spoken.*) We'll see if "tricking" is worth my time, and if I'll be lucky enough to get a good piece—It seems funny to me to have to put down money instead of receiving it. Fuck it! you have to experience everything in life, everything!

Scene Three

(*The action continues on the street. Dorante, walking in front of the house with the large number, meets Sylva who is pounding the pavement.*)

Sylvia. (*Stopping, her heart in her mouth.*) Pretty boy!

Dorante. (*Admiring the fullness of Sylvia's crinoline dress.*) Superb stew!

Sylvia. (*With a voice sweet as honey.*) Pretty boy, would you like to come to my place?—

Dorante. (*Seduced by Sylvia's turn of phrase, decidedly.*) Hey! Hey! I'm not saying no. (*Softly.*) Got to see this undressed— There may be more joy than meat underneath—

Sylvia. (*In a voice that becomes gradually more insinuating.*) Pretty boy, come with me. You won't be sorry. I'll be very nice—very naughty—You want it? Come!

Dorante. (*Allowing himself to be carried away; aside*) This creature carries herself well—It ought to be a good drop— However, when unpacking—I have so often been ripped off.

Sylvia. (*Leading him down the alley of the brothel, and taking advantage of the momentary darkness to put her hand on his cock.*) You're going to have fun, my darling, I won't disappoint you. (*They enter the brothel.*)

Scene Four

(*The action takes place in a small room in the brothel at Rez-de-Chausée. Once she has entered, Sylvia raises the wick of the lamp placed on the fireplace, but not too much, however, in order not to give away her make-up. Having taken care of this, she approaches Dorante and passes her hand several times over his crotch, to maintain the fire she believes she has kindled.*)

Dorante. I'd take something, myself—And you, with the beautiful thighs?

Sylvia. Looks like you've already got a hard-on—little pig! And I too would like to be licking a drink—What are you paying for, my love?

Dorante. Whatever you like—Go more slowly, eh? I don't have a spare—Gotta be careful with such fragile objects—

Sylvia. There—there—Don't be angry, darling. I'll go more as you please. You'll hardly feel me. It's true that you only have one—and that's a shame, isn't it? Why, by the way, is it that you don't have two? We have two nipples, ourselves!

Dorante. It's not the same thing, the damned beast!

Sylvia. You think? You might be right at that. I would whistle for an absinthe, what do you say, honey?

Dorante. Absinthe? Damn! You have good taste! Okay. Two absinthes!

Sylvia. (*While preparing the two glasses.*) So, you want to find happiness, little man?

Dorante. Yes, I've been itching in my pants since noon. It is ten o'clock—you decide if I ought to be suffering!

Sylvia. Poor kitty! Very well! You'll feel better, my darling, I promise you. King Louis-Philippe will never've been as happy as you will be. (*She clinks glasses with him, while rubbing him.*) To your health!

Dorante. And yours, my gal! (*They drink.*)

Sylvia. Say, pretty boy, if you want me to be very nice, you have to give me your little gift—you know, the gift we always give to little ladies—

Dorante. Gloves? When you have such pretty tiny hands? Really! They would spoil them.

Sylvia. You know very well, my puss, that it is the custom.—They are little reimbursements for us poor girls. Madame takes everything from us and gives us nothing. Come on, be generous.

Dorante. I'll stake you a hundred sous—but you'll do everything to me?

Sylvia. (*Her right hand is extended to take the money, her left hand is busy groping Dorante who permits it.*) Yes, whatever you want, everything. I'll be really naughty, you'll see. You can fuck me as much as you want. I'll jerk you off, I'll suck you, I'll let you ride me—you'll cum!—But give me your little gift.

Dorante. When I've cum— if you have been very nice. You make promises like that, you people, a lot of promises that you don't keep— It's like your nipples: they promise and never deliver—

Sylvia. Do you want me to take them out? I'll take them out. But give me your little gift.

Dorante. No—after!

Sylvia. No—before! You've got a nice package, my darling!

Dorante. No way—After—It's true, I've always been told that.

Sylvia. The women you fuck must be very happy! Come on, give me half of it?—So, you don't trust me?

Dorante. I trust, without being— Women are so deceptive! When you're at my rear door you'll think you're done by getting on your own and wiggling your ass for three minutes. I know that, my little mother!

(*Sings, to the tune of a song from* Fortunio.)

If you think I'm a novice,

You'll get the hang of it!

When you complete your service,

You'll have a hundred sous—

Sylvia. (*Sings, to the same tune.*)

Come on, give it to me in advance,

And you'll see!

Dorante. (*Same tune.*)

No—no—I don't trust you—

You'll cheat!

Cause I know these seesaws,

I'm a rogue,

And I could write the Memoirs

Of Lupanar–that house of prostitution!

Sylvia. (*Who pulled his cock out of his pants, and is jerking it off. Spoken.*) You? You're too good for that—

Dorante. (*Passing her his tongue. Spoken.*) You think?

Sylvia. (*Wiping her mouth, without abandoning his cock.*) Pig! You must be at least a stockbroker—

Dorante. Close. Will you make me the commissioner's hat—suck me off and play with my balls?

Sylvia. Since I told you that I would do anything for you! God, what a beautiful dick! Is this all yours, my darling?

Dorante. Who do you want it to belong to? The Grand Turk?

Sylvia. It's because you seem to have it for two. You're so well-built. My God! It makes you cum in your mouth! You should be well-suited for a woman, eh?

Dorante. You'll see. Let's go up!

Sylvia. (*Abandoning Dorante's prick to go unlock the door.*) No, let's stay here—no one will disturb us. God! My darling, you're so well-built. You're not an ordinary man!

Dorante. (*Who is thinking of everything, while planning to make his play.*) And the water—

Sylvia. (*Who has regained possession of his cock and who works it gently.*) What water? (*She runs her tongue over his dick.*) It's a real cock, at least!

Dorante. For washing. Don't you know how to use the toilet in this school?

Sylvia. Yes, my darling. Here, in this bathroom. Oh! Nothing's missing here. It's a good house. (*Aside.*) Fuck. He's a serious trick.

Dorante. I'll let you to start the commissioner's hat. By the way, what's your name?

Sylvia. (*Her mouth full.*) Sylvia, my darling.

Dorante. That's a nice name—Sylvia. Don't go too fast, bitch! I don't want to cum too fast. I like it to last a long time.

Sylvia. We'll start over, pretty boy. Don't you worry!—And you, what's your first name? Your bird name?

Dorante. (*Aside.*) Let's keep our true name from her. It is too well known. (*Aloud.* My name is Theodore. Does it suit you?

Sylvia. (*Still with her mouth full.*) It's a bourgeois name. I like it. Do you feel it's coming, my angel?

Dorante. I'll fart to warn you; it's my custom.

Sylvia. (*Stopping from sucking him, to catch a breath.*) Hey, you're funny, all the same!

Dorante. You don't say? But why did you stop blowing me? It was going well.

Sylvia. It was to catch a breath, my darling. If you like, we could have sex. It's better. Take off your pants.

Dorante. Why?

Sylvia. We have people who like it—it's more comfortable—

Dorante. Some bucks! I never take off my clothes, myself: I don't know what could happen.

Sylvia. Oh! the house is safe—In a word, opinions are liberal. Keep your pants on—that won't stop you from doing it to me, will it?

Dorante. You'll get first-rate attention, my Infanta! But if I don't take off my clothes, I'm not against someone taking off her dress when she wants to please me—

Sylvia. (*Eagerly undressing.*) My underwear, if you want!

Dorante. No, only your dress. Underwear is more arousing—I never have a good erection in front of a chick who is all naked—while the underwear is there, very white, with its hollows and its mountains, it gives me a rise down there. Let's go!

Sylvia. Sit down, my puss—I'll continue the big game—after the commissioner's hat, I'll ride you. (*She stands him up completely, pulls his shirt up and sticks her finger in his ass.*) Don't be afraid: my nails are clipped—What are you feeling, my angel?

Dorante. (*Impassive.*) Nothing.

Sylvia. I'm surprised. (*Sings, to the tune of "I have a wagging foot."*)

I have a wagging finger

Deep in your ass;

I have a wagging finger

Deep in your asshole.

Dorante. (*Sings, to the same tune.*)

My beauty,

Who gave you

This custom

That you have?

My beauty,

Who gave you

This custom

That you have?

Sylvia. (*Same tune.*)

Sir, it's my lover—

When I see him, my ass is very comfortable!

Sir, it's my lover—

When I see him, my ass is happy.

Dorante. (*Who, while erect, does not yet feel able to fuck. Spoken.*) Enough! Enough! I got my ass full of that tune and your finger—Something else, if you want to make me paddle for real; something else!

Sylvia. (*Aside, with astonishment.*) He doesn't ignite! However, I wouldn't mind having him fuck me, because he's got a rugged member!—(*Aloud*) You don't easily get the idea, my darling!

Dorante. I'm no fool! There are people who come to the brothel to take a piss, and who go back with the clap—me, I want to piss and shit, and if I catch something, at least I won't have been robbed—Show me pictures of holiness!

Sylvia. Yes, my dear—our house is not lacking for anything, I told you. (*She scrolls before her eyes a host of transparencies, which are as much an insult to good taste as to good morals, and while showing them to him, she supports herself with the hand she has left.*) Are you happy?

Dorante. (*Still impassive.*) No. I want my five senses to be satisfied. That's what I call the big game! Touch! you jerked me off; Smell? you gave me absinthe; Sight? I have contemplated this garbage (*Pointing to the pictures.*), and you. All I lack is the satisfaction of hearing and taste. (*Indicating the piano that adorns the living room.*) There's a cauldron; bang me something on it. Then we'll see—

Sylvia. (*Sitting down to the piano.*) I will do anything to please you, my angel. (*Aside, after throwing a last glance at Dorante's pants.*) What a beautiful cock! I can't take my eyes off it. Since that of Augustus, my rifleman, I've never seen one like it! What a dick! (*Sings, to a tune to be chosen.*)

In this silly banter
That produces voluptuousness,
The hole that a finger fondles
Is happy in truth;
But nothing goes to the head,
No, nothing is more mischievous
Than a tongue always ready
To lick the hole.
Sweetie-pie!
Sweetie-pie!
Oh, my God! Oh! that's good!

(*Spoken.*) And now, my lamb, it's up to you to do it. Make me a distinguished chick, worthy of the cum we are going to squirt together.

Dorante. Let's go! (*He rushes over to Sylvia, throws her down on the couch, rolls up her shirt, and works his tongue skillfully; then, when he has made her wiggle her buttocks and cum for her own sake, he substitutes his cock for his tongue, waggles her buttocks and cums on his own. Tableau.*)

Sylvia. (*While pouring water on his crotch and handing him a white towel to wipe off.*) You made me cum, you naughty boy! This is the first time that I came so easily and so honestly! And you, my angel, did you cum?

Dorante. (*After wiping his crotch, and buttoning up.*) Didn't you hear me fart?

Sylvia. So that's the way you announce your joy to women?

Dorante. Yes, that's how it is every time I pull up my cobblestones with a young lady—And now, chick, since I fucked your asshole, and fucked you as you've never been fucked in your fucking life, I have the honor to point out to you that you've been deceived. You stuck your finger in the eye up to your elbow!

Sylvia. (*Who thinks he is alluding to the butt-fucking.*) Oh! In the eye?—

Dorante. That's right. I forgot! In the eye—and in the other. I'm not a trick, my dear.

Sylvia. You're not a trick?

Dorante. To the contrary. I'm a pimp.

Sylvia. A pimp!—I should have guessed.

Dorante. Why?—

Sylvia. You haven't paid up yet!

Dorante. Well-discovered, but too late. Well! do you want me to tell you about yourself? You don't look like an ordinary streetwalker to me either—or you haven't been in the profession for long.

Sylvia. Why?

Dorante. You jerked me off, sucked, buttfucked, and you let yourself climb up the stairs, not only before I gave you your gloves, but before I even set the price for my hour of passion. If I had you in my brothel, I'd kick you out, so you don't give those damn habits to my girls.

Sylvia. That's true.—I'm pinched!

Dorante. Pinched? What do you mean?

Sylvia. I mean that you are a gallant fucker, that you suit me like never before—in fact, I have never been so well-suited, and that, if you agree to it, it won't be you who'll give me the cash, it is I who will be your pot—

Dorante. Would you be?—

Sylvia. I am the patroness of this bazaar, the mother of eighteen little ladies, for example, whom you will be forbidden to touch. Does that suit you?

Dorante. It fits me like a glove. I'm in the office today, seeing that I fucked you for free and you rinsed my pecker with a glass of Swiss Absinthe.—I wanted to taste different kinds of bread, but I see that a loaf of white bread is still the best.

Let's eat white! let's eat white!

Better than eating a custard tart!

Let's eat white until dawn,

And let Phoebus still finds us

Eating white!

Sylvia. Always clowning! Ah! I don't know when it will happen, but I'll have a proud hat for you, all right! You'll take it easy with me, I'll answer you in kind! (*She grabs his prick eagerly, like a woman who's still hungry.*) May we drink to our contract, eh?

Dorante. (*Acting eager, although deep down he's had enough for the moment.*) Let's drink to it!

(*She lays on her back again, and he sets out to fuck her. While the two of them are busy twitching and making the springs of the divan scream with their efforts, we hear the voices of policemen singing from the street to the tune of "Bourbaki's retreat."*)

Zealous officers, let's sing our rondeau well,

And capture

As much of the world

As we can;

In this way,

Through infractions,

In our position

We'll advance

And have pensions!

Sylvia. (*Who is about to cum, and who, despite this, does not lose sight of the interests of her brothel. Same tune.*)

(*Sings.*) Gentle—men, police—men, we are—very quiet;

We—are—sleeping,

And—all—our—girls

Are—with—their—tricks—

If you want,

I'll—open—the shutters;

So— you—can—enter,

And—fuck

Any—whomever—you want.

(*Speaking.*) Ah! Naughty boy! How well you do that!

Dorante. (*Removing cock and balls from under her dress, and ceasing to cum. The same tune.*)

Well answered! you know the fuzz well!

(*Sings.*) They won't let her

Stick them with a sweetheart

Who tires them out.

(*To the public.*)

Lovely audience,

Like gentlemen police,

In our establishment

You will be well-received

If you applaud!

The End.

The Grisette and the Student
(1863)
A play in one act
By Henry Monnier

The introduction for The Grisette and the Student *in* Le Théâtre Erotique de la rue de la Santé *reveals that "Henry Monnier energetically repudiated the authorship of this comedy. When he came to offer* The Grisette and the Student *to the administration of the Theatre in the rue de la Santé, Monnier was in his sixties. He himself made the three characters of the comedy speak.*

"He himself came to receive, with the constitutional imperturbability of an indurated show-off, the congratulations of idolatrous and virtuous spectators, including Paul Féval, Paul Blaquière, then melancholy and consumptive, Charles Bataille, Edmond Duranty, Albert Glatigny, etc., etc., over whom visibly hovered the shadows of all the eventual reporters of the Monthyon Prize (awarded by the French Academy of Sciences and the Académie française).

"The autograph manuscript of M. Henry Monnier, of which we are the happy owner, cannot, moreover, leave any doubt about the cohabitation in which this mournful rascal indulged with Mademoiselle Musa, in order to procreate The Grisette and the Student.

"Come on, Monnier, you are really wrong to deny your attempt at promiscuous comedy. It will count for more than the catch phrases with which you sadden the suppers where your place is marked as the author of The Lowlands; *and it is better, a thousand times over, than your play,* Painters and Bourgeois, *made in collaboration with an out-of-work traveling clerk, and which was such a funereal flop in the black vault of the Odéon Theatre.*

"Monnier gave two performances of The Grisette and the Student *at the Theatre in the rue de la Santé."*

Characters

The Student
The Grisette
The Voice of Mr. Prudhomme

(*The action takes place in a furnished room on Harpe Street in Paris in 1850 or earlier, in 1840 or later.*)

The Student. (*Reading a letter.*) "Tuesday, at noon, I'll be at your house, sooner than later. Love me always as I love you. Be wise and reasonable, but not too dirty-minded. If you want, we'll get into mischief." (*Spoken.*) Ten after eleven. She isn't coming. (*Rereading the letter.*) "Tuesday at noon." (*Spoken.*) She isn't late—Put out her chair—eleven thirty! (*Reading again.*) "I'll be at your house, sooner than later." (*Spoken.*) Quarter to twelve! (*He hears a knock at the door.*) Who is it?

A High Voice. Me!

The Student. (*Acting as if he does not recognize her voice.*) Who are you?

The Same High Voice. Me!! (*He opens the door. Enter the Grisette, red like a peony who has climbed up six floors.*)

The Grisette. Hello, my pet. How are you? God, it's high! I'm all out of breath—and the doorman who keeps asking me where I'm going—you understand that? He kept making me repeat it to let me come up—so I hate him, that old buffoon! Hug me? — Let me take off my hat.

The Student. (*With the eagerness of a man with an erection.*) Give it to me, my angel.

The Grisette. (*Removing her hat.*) Here—Do you love me, pussycat? Come, hug me.

The Student. (*Who has taken her in his arms.*) Yes—

The Grisette. (*Putting her face against her lover's lips.*) We'll be very wise—(*Surprised.*) My word!

The Student (*His dick harder than before, uses his tongue to kiss her.*) Yes—

The Grisette. Ah! Not like that, pussycat, not like that—Ah! You're a pig! Not the tongue, I beg you, not the tongue. Do you know what I have under my shawl?

The Student. (*Who is too erect to guess what it is.*) Suspenders that you embroidered?

The Grisette. (*Who, for a moment, eludes her lover's tongue, and who hops into the room like a wagtail.*) No. In a pot?

The Student. Suspenders—in a pot?

The Grisette. (*Bursts out laughing.*) You big silly! In the pot—it's the raisin bread my mother sent me for the winter. You like raisin bread, don't you, you big puss? We'll eat it.

The Student. (*Who is preoccupied with kissing the grisette.*) Yes—

The Grisette. (*Stopping in front of the fireplace.*) Hey! Where's your clock?

The Student. At the shop.

The Grisette. And the crystal, too? (*Changing the subject.*) She's at my aunt's.

The Student. I'm afraid so.

The Grisette. (*Sulking.*) Ah! Yes, I know—It was the other day, when you were in Meudon, with your Madame Machin, that you kept me waiting. (*With spirit.*) I had the exact amount of money—twenty-five francs—I was ready for you!

The Student. (*Who has managed to lure her into a chair.*) You bitch!

The Grisette. Kiss me, quickly, you bad boy—kiss me! (*He gives her a long French kiss.*) No—not like that, my pet, not like that—Please! Start over. No tricks, pussy cat! Please. (*He amorously pinches her ass.*) I don't want—no! Work—(*He glides through her breasts.*) No—leave me alone, I say—I've come here so that you can work. I'll sit down next to you. (*She leaps into an adjacent chair.*) Right!

Be nice! It's been a long time since I've seen you! Kiss me, you bad boy—kiss me better than that—tell me, does your Madame Marchin have as deep a throat as I?

The Student. (*Who has his hands full.*) Wow! Wow!

The Grisette. (*Arching her back to better protrude her tits.*) I'm certain that she doesn't have a set like mine. You won't find one like this every other day, you know, pussy cat. No! Your lady may be better dressed, but she doesn't have my body. Here! Look at my boobs—how fat they are. (*She displays them through an opening in her blouse.*) Do you like my apples? (*He plays with them with his finger and his tongue.*) Oh! No—don't touch them, sir! I want to preserve them for a long time. No, please—Ah!—No—pussy cat—no—Work—Ah! Pig!—

The Student. (*Pulling her on to her knees and rolling her dress up.*) I'm working too.

The Grisette. (*Defending herself weakly.*) Not that kind of work—I want you to be reasonable (*He spreads her thighs.*) Okay! Okay! Where are you going with this? What are you stuffing down there? Ah! Like you're a pig—like a pig! It's not what I want—no—I know you: after you've done it, you send me away—No! Please! No—I'm telling you—pussy cat—No! No! Not like that—it pinches my stomach. (*He masturbates her.*) Not my hole—my little hole—that's better! Ah! Yes! (*With a languid voice.*) Work—

The Student. (*Replacing his finger with his prick.*) I'll work after—

The Grisette. (*Who begins to show the whites of her eyes.*) No, pussy cat—you know very well what you did the other time—No! Oh, no! Must you always give in? Yes—you want to do it—Ah!

The Student. (*Thrusting his prick.*) Yes—

The Grisette. On the bed, my pet—on the bed—it's a better place for this— (*He carries her to the bed and begins the assault with a certain intensity.*) Wait—wait until I take my dress off. You want to see me naked! Look—here I am! Go on— Not like that! You're going in the wrong hole. Let me direct it—Nope!—Wait, my little man—Oh!—wait. Let's take our time with this—a very long time. Isn't that right, my pet? There you are. Do you feel me?

The Student. (*Vigorously thrusting his crotch.*) Yes—

The Grisette. (*Happily, unable to hold back her joyful sighs that resemble groans.*) Han! Han! Han! Oh, that's good! I enjoy it. Go! Han!—Ah! That's good—

The Student. (*Enjoying it as well, but more silently.*) Dear angel! I love you!—

The Grisette. (*Responding to her lover's cock thrusts by as many ass thrusts.*) You—will—al—ways—love—me—?

The Student. (*Who is still in the saddle.*) Yes—

The Grisette. (*Crying out, in a paroxysm of joy.*) Go on! Go! Go! little man—Not right away—Not yet—Ah! It's coming—You got me wet—Ah! How enjoyable! My God, how enjoyable! It goes all the way to the roots of my hair—Ah!—yes! Kill me! Ah! Kill me—Ah! Kill me!

The Voice of Mr. Prudhomme. No murders in the house, if you please! Eh? In there, will you soon be finished with your depravities?

The Grisette. (*Still wriggling.*) Who's that next door?

The Voice of Mr. Prudhomme. You're going to bring me to regrettable attacks upon my person—(*The two lovers, who haven't quite finished yet, do not breathe a word; the bed alone speaks for them, eloquently.*)

The Grisette. (*In the final convulsions of happiness.*) Who's that next door?

The Student. (*Still rubbing his dick, to ease his conscience, since he no longer has a hard-on.*) An old bastard!—

The Grisette. (*Still aroused.*) We were doing so well—I would like to start over—And you, pussy cat?

The Student. (*Masturbating her, to give his cock a breather.*) Me too—

The Grisette. (*Who is for enjoyment that's serious, not for what is nearly so.*) Not like that! Polyte, my Lilyte, take out your hand—take out your hand. No! I don't want—Take out your hand—please!

The Voice of Mr. Prudhomme. Hippolyte, take out your hand!

The Student. (*To Mr. Prudhomme.*) You're not going to fucking leave us alone, you—

The Voice of Mr. Prudhomme. Very well, sir. You've gotten me out of bed. I'm leaving the room. I'm going to finish my nap in an adjoining bedroom, while you finish your fornicating in yours.

The Student. Finally, that idiot is gone—What were we saying before?

The Grisette. (*Who does not lose sight of her subject or his hand.*) We were saying, pussy cat, that we were being silly. I would like to kiss you. Give me a little peck. (*Groping his balls, and tickling his cock.*) I want to see if you're in the mood—(*Noticing that he's erect.*) Yes, you're in the mood, you pig! (*With admiration, and wanting to take advantage of the situation.*) It's stronger than it was earlier—And hard! It feels like iron! How does such a big deal not hit the stomach when it goes in? (*She greedily grabs it and puts it inside her.*) Wait, my pet, wait—That's fine for now—Go on! Ah! Mama! Ah! Mama! Mama!

The Student. (*Who enjoys more silently, but just as deeply.*) Ah! Dear angel! Dear angel!—

The Grisette. (*Swimming in a lake of ecstasy.*) Oh! Go! Go! Go now! Push, man, push! Come on, push! Ah! How good you feel! Ah! Mama, mama, that's good! How well you do that, my sweet—Are you as happy as I am? Speak to me, please—Ah! Oh, that's good! Say you love me—but—there—good!

The Student. (*Still thrusting.*) Yes—

The Grisette. (*Her buttocks squirming.*) Say it yourself—

The Student. I love you.

The Grisette. (*Begging.*) Give me your tongue—your nice, sweet, little tongue—(*Imperiously.*) Your tongue! Your tongue! Ah! My twink—Ah! Ah! Ah!—

The Student. My chickadee—

The Grisette. (*Enraptured.*) Your chickadee. Yes—your little darling hen. Your—your—hen—darling—

The Student. Yes—

The Grisette. (*Acting like a nut-cracker.*) Do you feel like I'm hugging you? Go deeper—to the very bottom—Push, little man—push. You'll tell me when you're going to come—

The Student. (*Hastening his thrusts.*) Yes—

The Grisette. (*Pleading.*) Not without me! Not without me! Together! Enjoy—let's enjoy it—together—good—together! Oh! Mama! Mama! Mama! Oh, that's good! Kill me! Kill me! Kill me! Oh!

The Student. (*Who has ejaculated.*) Yes—

The Grisette. (*Clutching hands and feet.*) Ah! Ah! Ah! I enjoyed that—yes! And you, pussy cat? You—?

The Student. (*Pulling out his cock.*) Me too—

The Grisette. (*With reproach.*) Ah! You pulled out! Why didn't you stay inside me? I wouldn't have eaten it! Come on! Lie again like before—there—our stomachs touching—Already finished! Ah! That's ridiculous! It should last a lifetime—

(*Silence. The two lovers, still entwined, peck each other tenderly, but without thrusting their hips. The grisette presses the student forcefully against her breasts, sighing and quivering, experiencing the last shivers of pleasure; after a while, she begins again; her hand, already bouncing under her lover's balls, is about to tickle them and awaken their sleeping sperm; but the student, who has only two shots to his bow, abruptly evades this prompting, by jumping from the bed.*)

The Student. Didn't I tell you I had to go out?

The Grisette. (*Surprised.*) No. See how you're a pig—when you're through with me, you throw me out! It's always the same tune—

The Student. Because I have to go out.

The Grisette. (*Still on the bed, and crying hot tears.*) Hi! Hi! Hi! Hi! Hi!

The Student. (*Annoyed.*) Ah! If you cry, we're going to have a lot of fun.

The Grisette. (*Still crying.*) I who mattered so long as we went out together! Hi! Hi! Hi!

The Student. (*Impatiently.*) Because I'm telling you that I have to run an errand for my mother!

The Grisette. So, your mother just arrived?

The Student. Didn't I tell you?

The Grisette. You told me the last time. Ah! I'm not happy! No. I have no luck. It's like the dress you promised me—

The Student. You'll get it—

The Grisette. (*Jumping off the bed.*) When? In a month of Sundays, right?

The Student. (*Going to his desk.*) Here's your dress! (*He angrily throws her a twenty-franc note.*)

The Grisette. (*Bursting with sadness.*) This is not how I wanted it! Not like this! Ah, my God!—my God! (*She sobs and swoons.*)

The Student. (*Running to her.*) Well! What! You're going to feel bad now! Fanny! Fanny! Poor darling pussy. Answer me—Fanny! Fanny! Please! (*He takes her in his arms and tenderly caresses her.*) You're crying! Fie! How ugly! Will you quickly wipe away those nasty tears!

The Grisette. (*Laughing out of one eye and still crying in the other.*) No! I'll continue to cry—and laugh—look! And you too—you cried. Fuck me and be rougher, pussy cat. You want more, more of everything!

The End.

A Select Bibliography

Capon, Gaston and R. Yve-Plessis. *Paris Galant au Dix-Huitième Siècle: Les Théâtres clandestins.* Paris: Plessis, 1905.

Hunt, Lynn, ed. *The Invention of Pornography: Obscenity and the Origins of Modernity, 1500–1800.* New York: Zone Books, 1996.

Marchand, Henry L. *The Erotic History of France.* N.p.: Panurge Press, 1933.

Monnier, Henry. *Le Théâtre Erotique de la rue de la Santé: son histoire.* Batignolles: N.p., 1864–1866.

Nelson, Ida. *La Sottie sans souci: Essai d'interprétation homosexuelle.* Paris: Editions Honoré Champion, 1977.

Smith, Daniel T., Jr. "Libertine dramaturgy: Reading obscene closet drama in eighteenth-century France" (UMI Number: 3402248). [Dissertation, Northwestern University]. UMI, 2010.

Théâtre Erotique Français au XVIIIe siècle. Paris: Jean-Jacques Pauvert au Terrain Vague, 1993.

Le Théâtre gaillard, revu et augmenté, 1776–1865. 2 vols. Reprint. Ann Arbor: MLibrary, 2020.

Rochester, John Wilmot, Earl of. *Sodom, or the Quintessence of Debauchery.* C.1725. Reprint. Hollywood: Brandon House, 1966.